TEACHER'S PET PUBLICATIONS

PUZZLE PACK
for
Pygmalion

based on the play by
George Bernard Shaw

Written by
William T. Collins

© 2005 Teacher's Pet Publications
All Rights Reserved

The materials in this packet are copyrighted
by Teacher's Pet Publications, Inc.

These pages may be duplicated by the purchaser
for use in the purchaser's own classroom.

Copying any of these materials and distributing them
for any other purpose is a violation of the copyright laws.

© 2005 Teacher's Pet Publications, Inc.
www.tpet.com

INTRODUCTION
If you already own the LitPlan for this title, this Puzzle Pack will refresh your Unit Resource Materials and Vocabulary Resource Materials sections plus give you additional materials you can substitute into the tests. If you do not already have a complete LitPlan, these pages will give you some supplemental materials to use with your own plan. There are two main groups of materials: one set for unit words (such as characters' names, symbols, places, etc.) and one set for vocabulary words associated with the book.

WORD LIST
There is a word list for both the unit words and the vocabulary words. These lists show you which words are being used in the materials and the clues or definitions being used for those words. You may want to give students a word list with clues/definitions to help them, or you may want students to only have a word list (without clues/definitions) if you want them to work a little harder. Both are available for duplication. The word lists can also be your "calling key" for the bingo games.

FILL IN THE BLANK AND MATCHING
There are 4 each of the fill in the blank and matching worksheets for both the unit and vocabulary words. These pages can be used either as extra worksheets for students or as objective parts of a unit test. They can be done individually if students need extra help or as a whole class activity to review the material covered.

MAGIC SQUARES
The magic squares not only reinforce the material covered but also work on reasoning and math skills. Many teachers have told us that their students really enjoy doing these!

WORD SEARCH PUZZLES
The word search words go in all directions, as indicated on your answer keys. Two of the word search puzzles have the clues listed rather than the words. This makes the puzzle a little more difficult, but it reinforces the material better. Two word search puzzles have words only for students who find the clue puzzles too difficult.

CROSSWORD PUZZLES
Both unit and vocabulary word sections have 4 crossword puzzles.

BINGO CARDS
There are 32 individual bingo cards for the unit words and 32 individual bingo cards for the vocabulary words. You can use your word list as a "call list," calling the words at random and marking them off of your list as you go, or you could use the flash cards by cutting them apart and drawing the words at random from a hat (or box or whatever). To make a better review, you might ask for the definition and spelling of each word as you call it out–or you could call out the definitions and have students tell you the words they need to look for on the puzzle.

JUGGLE LETTERS
The vocabulary juggle letter game is intended to help students learn the spellings of the words. One sheet has the definitions listed on it as an extra help for students who need it or to reinforce the definitions if you choose to do so.

FLASH CARDS
We've included a set of vocabulary flash cards you can duplicate, cut, and fold for your students. Some teachers make a few sets for general use by the class; others make a set for each student. Some teachers duplicate them for each student and have the students cut & fold their own. You can cut out just the words and put them in a hat, have each student pick out one word and write the definition and a sentence for that word. Students then swap words and papers, with the next student adding a sentence of his own under the last one. You can have students swap as many times as you like. Each time the student will read the sentences written prior to his own and then add a sentence. You can cut out the words and definitions separately and play "I Have; Who Has?" Each student in the room draws a word and definition. The first student says, "I have (the name of the word). Who has the definition?" The student with the definition reads it then says, "I have (the name of the vocabulary word she has). Who has the definition?" The round continues until all words and definitions have been given.

Pygmalion Word List

No.	Word	Clue/Definition
1.	ACT	Play division
2.	ALFRED	This Doolittle tried to blackmail Higgins.
3.	AMBASSADOR	He had a reception
4.	CLARA	Tries to imitate Liza's manners
5.	DIGNITY	Liza has this; sense of personal self-worth
6.	DOOLITTLE	Eliza's last name
7.	DUSTBIN	'She's deliciously low--so horribly dirty....Put her in the_____'
8.	EYNSFORD	____ - Hill; mother and daughter from the rainstorm in Act One
9.	FAIR	My ____ Lady; musical version of Pygmalion
10.	FLOWERS	Eliza sold these
11.	FREDDY	Eliza marries him
12.	HIGGINS	The professor who transforms Liza
13.	IMAGINATION	It's only ____. Low spirits and nothing else.
14.	LADY	Gentlewoman
15.	LIZA	Flower girl who becomes a lady
16.	MANNERS	Social graces
17.	MYSELF	I sold flowers. I didn't sell ___.
18.	NATURAL	I only want to be ___.
19.	NEPOMMUCK	Guest at ambassador's reception who was fluent in many languages
20.	PEARCE	Housekeeper for Higgins
21.	PICKERING	The colonel
22.	PYGMALION	He created a statue of a woman so beautiful he fell in love with her
23.	RAIN	Gives the characters a believable motivation for meeting
24.	RESPONSIBILITY	Alfred wanted a life free of this.
25.	RICH	Having lots of money
26.	SCENE	Act division
27.	SHAW	Author
28.	SHOP	Liza gets her own flower ____
29.	SLIPPERS	Liza throws Higgins' ____ at him
30.	SPEECH	Higgins and Pickering both study this
31.	STAGE	Place where play is usually performed
32.	TROUBLE	Making life means making ___.
33.	VULGAR	Kind of language Eliza uses to tell the story of her aunt's death

Pygmalion Fill In The Blanks 1

_____   1. Liza gets her own flower ____
_____   2. Eliza sold these
_____   3. Act division
_____   4. Play division
_____   5. Place where play is usually performed
_____   6. Flower girl who becomes a lady
_____   7. The colonel
_____   8. I only want to be ___.
_____   9. Liza has this; sense of personal self-worth
_____   10. Housekeeper for Higgins
_____   11. Guest at ambassador's reception who was fluent in many languages
_____   12. Gentlewoman
_____   13. Kind of language Eliza uses to tell the story of her aunt's death
_____   14. Eliza's last name
_____   15. Author
_____   16. I sold flowers. I didn't sell ___.
_____   17. Tries to imitate Liza's manners
_____   18. ____ - Hill; mother and daughter from the rainstorm in Act One
_____   19. Alfred wanted a life free of this.
_____   20. Liza throws Higgins' ____ at him

Pygmalion Fill In The Blanks 1 Answer Key

SHOP	1. Liza gets her own flower ____
FLOWERS	2. Eliza sold these
SCENE	3. Act division
ACT	4. Play division
STAGE	5. Place where play is usually performed
LIZA	6. Flower girl who becomes a lady
PICKERING	7. The colonel
NATURAL	8. I only want to be ____.
DIGNITY	9. Liza has this; sense of personal self-worth
PEARCE	10. Housekeeper for Higgins
NEPOMMUCK	11. Guest at ambassador's reception who was fluent in many languages
LADY	12. Gentlewoman
VULGAR	13. Kind of language Eliza uses to tell the story of her aunt's death
DOOLITTLE	14. Eliza's last name
SHAW	15. Author
MYSELF	16. I sold flowers. I didn't sell ____.
CLARA	17. Tries to imitate Liza's manners
EYNSFORD	18. ____ - Hill; mother and daughter from the rainstorm in Act One
RESPONSIBILITY	19. Alfred wanted a life free of this.
SLIPPERS	20. Liza throws Higgins' ____ at him

Pygmalion Fill In The Blanks 2

1. I only want to be ____.
2. Gives the characters a believable motivation for meeting
3. He had a reception
4. The professor who transforms Liza
5. He created a statue of a woman so beautiful he fell in love with her
6. Having lots of money
7. It's only ____. Low spirits and nothing else.
8. Liza throws Higgins' ____ at him
9. Place where play is usually performed
10. Eliza's last name
11. Play division
12. Eliza marries him
13. Eliza sold these
14. Liza gets her own flower ____
15. Alfred wanted a life free of this.
16. Author
17. Social graces
18. My ____ Lady; musical version of Pygmalion
19. Guest at ambassador's reception who was fluent in many languages
20. Making life means making ____.

Pygmalion Fill In The Blanks 2 Answer Key

NATURAL	1. I only want to be ___.
RAIN	2. Gives the characters a believable motivation for meeting
AMBASSADOR	3. He had a reception
HIGGINS	4. The professor who transforms Liza
PYGMALION	5. He created a statue of a woman so beautiful he fell in love with her
RICH	6. Having lots of money
IMAGINATION	7. It's only ____. Low spirits and nothing else.
SLIPPERS	8. Liza throws Higgins' ____ at him
STAGE	9. Place where play is usually performed
DOOLITTLE	10. Eliza's last name
ACT	11. Play division
FREDDY	12. Eliza marries him
FLOWERS	13. Eliza sold these
SHOP	14. Liza gets her own flower ____
RESPONSIBILITY	15. Alfred wanted a life free of this.
SHAW	16. Author
MANNERS	17. Social graces
FAIR	18. My ____ Lady; musical version of Pygmalion
NEPOMMUCK	19. Guest at ambassador's reception who was fluent in many languages
TROUBLE	20. Making life means making ___.

Pygmalion Fill In The Blanks 3

_____   1. Social graces

_____   2. Liza has this; sense of personal self-worth

_____   3. Alfred wanted a life free of this.

_____   4. Guest at ambassador's reception who was fluent in many languages

_____   5. He had a reception

_____   6. Author

_____   7. Kind of language Eliza uses to tell the story of her aunt's death

_____   8. Liza gets her own flower ____

_____   9. This Doolittle tried to blackmail Higgins.

_____   10. Flower girl who becomes a lady

_____   11. Higgins and Pickering both study this

_____   12. Eliza's last name

_____   13. I only want to be ___.

_____   14. Making life means making ___.

_____   15. It's only ____. Low spirits and nothing else.

_____   16. Play division

_____   17. ____ - Hill; mother and daughter from the rainstorm in Act One

_____   18. Tries to imitate Liza's manners

_____   19. Housekeeper for Higgins

_____   20. Having lots of money

Pygmalion Fill In The Blanks 3 Answer Key

MANNERS	1. Social graces
DIGNITY	2. Liza has this; sense of personal self-worth
RESPONSIBILITY	3. Alfred wanted a life free of this.
NEPOMMUCK	4. Guest at ambassador's reception who was fluent in many languages
AMBASSADOR	5. He had a reception
SHAW	6. Author
VULGAR	7. Kind of language Eliza uses to tell the story of her aunt's death
SHOP	8. Liza gets her own flower ____
ALFRED	9. This Doolittle tried to blackmail Higgins.
LIZA	10. Flower girl who becomes a lady
SPEECH	11. Higgins and Pickering both study this
DOOLITTLE	12. Eliza's last name
NATURAL	13. I only want to be ___.
TROUBLE	14. Making life means making ___.
IMAGINATION	15. It's only ____. Low spirits and nothing else.
ACT	16. Play division
EYNSFORD	17. ____ - Hill; mother and daughter from the rainstorm in Act One
CLARA	18. Tries to imitate Liza's manners
PEARCE	19. Housekeeper for Higgins
RICH	20. Having lots of money

Pygmalion Fill In The Blanks 4

_____ 1. Gentlewoman

_____ 2. Housekeeper for Higgins

_____ 3. Flower girl who becomes a lady

_____ 4. Gives the characters a believable motivation for meeting

_____ 5. Alfred wanted a life free of this.

_____ 6. He had a reception

_____ 7. Liza has this; sense of personal self-worth

_____ 8. Place where play is usually performed

_____ 9. Guest at ambassador's reception who was fluent in many languages

_____ 10. Eliza sold these

_____ 11. Tries to imitate Liza's manners

_____ 12. The professor who transforms Liza

_____ 13. I sold flowers. I didn't sell ___.

_____ 14. Author

_____ 15. Kind of language Eliza uses to tell the story of her aunt's death

_____ 16. ____ - Hill; mother and daughter from the rainstorm in Act One

_____ 17. Eliza's last name

_____ 18. Social graces

_____ 19. This Doolittle tried to blackmail Higgins.

_____ 20. Making life means making ___.

Pygmalion Fill In The Blanks 4 Answer Key

Answer	#	Clue
LADY	1.	Gentlewoman
PEARCE	2.	Housekeeper for Higgins
LIZA	3.	Flower girl who becomes a lady
RAIN	4.	Gives the characters a believable motivation for meeting
RESPONSIBILITY	5.	Alfred wanted a life free of this.
AMBASSADOR	6.	He had a reception
DIGNITY	7.	Liza has this; sense of personal self-worth
STAGE	8.	Place where play is usually performed
NEPOMMUCK	9.	Guest at ambassador's reception who was fluent in many languages
FLOWERS	10.	Eliza sold these
CLARA	11.	Tries to imitate Liza's manners
HIGGINS	12.	The professor who transforms Liza
MYSELF	13.	I sold flowers. I didn't sell ___.
SHAW	14.	Author
VULGAR	15.	Kind of language Eliza uses to tell the story of her aunt's death
EYNSFORD	16.	___ - Hill; mother and daughter from the rainstorm in Act One
DOOLITTLE	17.	Eliza's last name
MANNERS	18.	Social graces
ALFRED	19.	This Doolittle tried to blackmail Higgins.
TROUBLE	20.	Making life means making ___.

Pygmalion Matching 1

___ 1. RESPONSIBILITY   A. Gives the characters a believable motivation for meeting
___ 2. TROUBLE   B. Eliza sold these
___ 3. SPEECH   C. My ____ Lady; musical version of Pygmalion
___ 4. FLOWERS   D. Tries to imitate Liza's manners
___ 5. AMBASSADOR   E. Alfred wanted a life free of this.
___ 6. IMAGINATION   F. Place where play is usually performed
___ 7. NATURAL   G. Eliza marries him
___ 8. DUSTBIN   H. Gentlewoman
___ 9. LADY   I. Higgins and Pickering both study this
___10. CLARA   J. He had a reception
___11. HIGGINS   K. The professor who transforms Liza
___12. SCENE   L. 'She's deliciously low--so horribly dirty....Put her in the____'
___13. RAIN   M. I only want to be ___.
___14. SHAW   N. ____ - Hill; mother and daughter from the rainstorm in Act One
___15. DOOLITTLE   O. I sold flowers. I didn't sell ___.
___16. PYGMALION   P. Guest at ambassador's reception who was fluent in many languages
___17. PEARCE   Q. Eliza's last name
___18. VULGAR   R. He created a statue of a woman so beautiful he fell in love with her
___19. FAIR   S. It's only ____. Low spirits and nothing else.
___20. MYSELF   T. Having lots of money
___21. FREDDY   U. Author
___22. RICH   V. Making life means making ___.
___23. NEPOMMUCK   W. Housekeeper for Higgins
___24. STAGE   X. Act division
___25. EYNSFORD   Y. Kind of language Eliza uses to tell the story of her aunt's death

Pygmalion Matching 1 Answer Key

E - 1. RESPONSIBILITY	A. Gives the characters a believable motivation for meeting
V - 2. TROUBLE	B. Eliza sold these
I - 3. SPEECH	C. My ____ Lady; musical version of Pygmalion
B - 4. FLOWERS	D. Tries to imitate Liza's manners
J - 5. AMBASSADOR	E. Alfred wanted a life free of this.
S - 6. IMAGINATION	F. Place where play is usually performed
M - 7. NATURAL	G. Eliza marries him
L - 8. DUSTBIN	H. Gentlewoman
H - 9. LADY	I. Higgins and Pickering both study this
D - 10. CLARA	J. He had a reception
K - 11. HIGGINS	K. The professor who transforms Liza
X - 12. SCENE	L. 'She's deliciously low--so horribly dirty....Put her in the_____'
A - 13. RAIN	M. I only want to be ___.
U - 14. SHAW	N. ____ - Hill; mother and daughter from the rainstorm in Act One
Q - 15. DOOLITTLE	O. I sold flowers. I didn't sell ___.
R - 16. PYGMALION	P. Guest at ambassador's reception who was fluent in many languages
W - 17. PEARCE	Q. Eliza's last name
Y - 18. VULGAR	R. He created a statue of a woman so beautiful he fell in love with her
C - 19. FAIR	S. It's only ____. Low spirits and nothing else.
O - 20. MYSELF	T. Having lots of money
G - 21. FREDDY	U. Author
T - 22. RICH	V. Making life means making ___.
P - 23. NEPOMMUCK	W. Housekeeper for Higgins
F - 24. STAGE	X. Act division
N - 25. EYNSFORD	Y. Kind of language Eliza uses to tell the story of her aunt's death

Pygmalion Matching 2

___ 1. SCENE   A. My _____ Lady; musical version of Pygmalion
___ 2. FAIR   B. Social graces
___ 3. PYGMALION   C. Eliza's last name
___ 4. ALFRED   D. Play division
___ 5. PEARCE   E. Liza gets her own flower _____
___ 6. LADY   F. Gentlewoman
___ 7. HIGGINS   G. Housekeeper for Higgins
___ 8. DUSTBIN   H. 'She's deliciously low--so horribly dirty....Put her in the_____'
___ 9. TROUBLE   I. He had a reception
___ 10. PICKERING   J. Act division
___ 11. CLARA   K. Eliza sold these
___ 12. FREDDY   L. Alfred wanted a life free of this.
___ 13. AMBASSADOR   M. Liza has this; sense of personal self-worth
___ 14. MANNERS   N. Higgins and Pickering both study this
___ 15. LIZA   O. Making life means making ___.
___ 16. VULGAR   P. Flower girl who becomes a lady
___ 17. FLOWERS   Q. Kind of language Eliza uses to tell the story of her aunt's death
___ 18. SHOP   R. Eliza marries him
___ 19. ACT   S. He created a statue of a woman so beautiful he fell in love with her
___ 20. DIGNITY   T. Liza throws Higgins' _____ at him
___ 21. RESPONSIBILITY U. This Doolittle tried to blackmail Higgins.
___ 22. DOOLITTLE   V. Gives the characters a believable motivation for meeting
___ 23. SLIPPERS   W. Tries to imitate Liza's manners
___ 24. RAIN   X. The colonel
___ 25. SPEECH   Y. The professor who transforms Liza

Pygmalion Matching 2 Answer Key

J - 1. SCENE	A.	My ____ Lady; musical version of Pygmalion
A - 2. FAIR	B.	Social graces
S - 3. PYGMALION	C.	Eliza's last name
U - 4. ALFRED	D.	Play division
G - 5. PEARCE	E.	Liza gets her own flower ____
F - 6. LADY	F.	Gentlewoman
Y - 7. HIGGINS	G.	Housekeeper for Higgins
H - 8. DUSTBIN	H.	'She's deliciously low--so horribly dirty....Put her in the ____'
O - 9. TROUBLE	I.	He had a reception
X - 10. PICKERING	J.	Act division
W - 11. CLARA	K.	Eliza sold these
R - 12. FREDDY	L.	Alfred wanted a life free of this.
I - 13. AMBASSADOR	M.	Liza has this; sense of personal self-worth
B - 14. MANNERS	N.	Higgins and Pickering both study this
P - 15. LIZA	O.	Making life means making ____.
Q - 16. VULGAR	P.	Flower girl who becomes a lady
K - 17. FLOWERS	Q.	Kind of language Eliza uses to tell the story of her aunt's death
E - 18. SHOP	R.	Eliza marries him
D - 19. ACT	S.	He created a statue of a woman so beautiful he fell in love with her
M - 20. DIGNITY	T.	Liza throws Higgins' ____ at him
L - 21. RESPONSIBILITY	U.	This Doolittle tried to blackmail Higgins.
C - 22. DOOLITTLE	V.	Gives the characters a believable motivation for meeting
T - 23. SLIPPERS	W.	Tries to imitate Liza's manners
V - 24. RAIN	X.	The colonel
N - 25. SPEECH	Y.	The professor who transforms Liza

Pygmalion Matching 3

___ 1. PICKERING
___ 2. NATURAL
___ 3. FREDDY
___ 4. CLARA
___ 5. HIGGINS
___ 6. SLIPPERS
___ 7. LIZA
___ 8. IMAGINATION
___ 9. SHAW
___10. EYNSFORD
___11. FLOWERS
___12. VULGAR
___13. MANNERS
___14. STAGE
___15. TROUBLE
___16. SCENE
___17. LADY
___18. RICH
___19. RAIN
___20. PEARCE
___21. RESPONSIBILITY
___22. AMBASSADOR
___23. PYGMALION
___24. ALFRED
___25. SPEECH

A. Flower girl who becomes a lady
B. He created a statue of a woman so beautiful he fell in love with her
C. Making life means making ___.
D. He had a reception
E. Tries to imitate Liza's manners
F. The colonel
G. It's only ____. Low spirits and nothing else.
H. Author
I. Place where play is usually performed
J. Gives the characters a believable motivation for meeting
K. The professor who transforms Liza
L. Liza throws Higgins' ____ at him
M. Having lots of money
N. Social graces
O. Act division
P. Kind of language Eliza uses to tell the story of her aunt's death
Q. Housekeeper for Higgins
R. Gentlewoman
S. Higgins and Pickering both study this
T. This Doolittle tried to blackmail Higgins.
U. I only want to be ___.
V. Alfred wanted a life free of this.
W. Eliza marries him
X. Eliza sold these
Y. ____ - Hill; mother and daughter from the rainstorm in Act One

Pygmalion Matching 3 Answer Key

F - 1. PICKERING	A.	Flower girl who becomes a lady
U - 2. NATURAL	B.	He created a statue of a woman so beautiful he fell in love with her
W - 3. FREDDY	C.	Making life means making ____.
E - 4. CLARA	D.	He had a reception
K - 5. HIGGINS	E.	Tries to imitate Liza's manners
L - 6. SLIPPERS	F.	The colonel
A - 7. LIZA	G.	It's only ____. Low spirits and nothing else.
G - 8. IMAGINATION	H.	Author
H - 9. SHAW	I.	Place where play is usually performed
Y -10. EYNSFORD	J.	Gives the characters a believable motivation for meeting
X -11. FLOWERS	K.	The professor who transforms Liza
P -12. VULGAR	L.	Liza throws Higgins' ____ at him
N -13. MANNERS	M.	Having lots of money
I -14. STAGE	N.	Social graces
C -15. TROUBLE	O.	Act division
O -16. SCENE	P.	Kind of language Eliza uses to tell the story of her aunt's death
R -17. LADY	Q.	Housekeeper for Higgins
M -18. RICH	R.	Gentlewoman
J -19. RAIN	S.	Higgins and Pickering both study this
Q -20. PEARCE	T.	This Doolittle tried to blackmail Higgins.
V -21. RESPONSIBILITY	U.	I only want to be ____.
D -22. AMBASSADOR	V.	Alfred wanted a life free of this.
B -23. PYGMALION	W.	Eliza marries him
T -24. ALFRED	X.	Eliza sold these
S -25. SPEECH	Y.	____ - Hill; mother and daughter from the rainstorm in Act One

Pygmalion Matching 4

___ 1. EYNSFORD
___ 2. SHOP
___ 3. DIGNITY
___ 4. DOOLITTLE
___ 5. RAIN
___ 6. FAIR
___ 7. RESPONSIBILITY
___ 8. DUSTBIN
___ 9. PEARCE
___ 10. RICH
___ 11. LIZA
___ 12. SHAW
___ 13. PYGMALION
___ 14. ACT
___ 15. PICKERING
___ 16. MYSELF
___ 17. AMBASSADOR
___ 18. IMAGINATION
___ 19. STAGE
___ 20. LADY
___ 21. SLIPPERS
___ 22. FREDDY
___ 23. SPEECH
___ 24. HIGGINS
___ 25. MANNERS

A. Alfred wanted a life free of this.
B. My ____ Lady; musical version of Pygmalion
C. The colonel
D. Author
E. Higgins and Pickering both study this
F. Flower girl who becomes a lady
G. The professor who transforms Liza
H. I sold flowers. I didn't sell ____.
I. Place where play is usually performed
J. Eliza marries him
K. ____ - Hill; mother and daughter from the rainstorm in Act One
L. Liza has this; sense of personal self-worth
M. Housekeeper for Higgins
N. He had a reception
O. He created a statue of a woman so beautiful he fell in love with her
P. Play division
Q. 'She's deliciously low--so horribly dirty....Put her in the____'
R. Liza throws Higgins' ____ at him
S. Having lots of money
T. It's only ____. Low spirits and nothing else.
U. Liza gets her own flower ____
V. Eliza's last name
W. Gentlewoman
X. Gives the characters a believable motivation for meeting
Y. Social graces

Pygmalion Matching 4 Answer Key

K - 1. EYNSFORD	A.	Alfred wanted a life free of this.
U - 2. SHOP	B.	My ____ Lady; musical version of Pygmalion
L - 3. DIGNITY	C.	The colonel
V - 4. DOOLITTLE	D.	Author
X - 5. RAIN	E.	Higgins and Pickering both study this
B - 6. FAIR	F.	Flower girl who becomes a lady
A - 7. RESPONSIBILITY	G.	The professor who transforms Liza
Q - 8. DUSTBIN	H.	I sold flowers. I didn't sell ___.
M - 9. PEARCE	I.	Place where play is usually performed
S - 10. RICH	J.	Eliza marries him
F - 11. LIZA	K.	____ - Hill; mother and daughter from the rainstorm in Act One
D - 12. SHAW	L.	Liza has this; sense of personal self-worth
O - 13. PYGMALION	M.	Housekeeper for Higgins
P - 14. ACT	N.	He had a reception
C - 15. PICKERING	O.	He created a statue of a woman so beautiful he fell in love with her
H - 16. MYSELF	P.	Play division
N - 17. AMBASSADOR	Q.	'She's deliciously low--so horribly dirty....Put her in the_____'
T - 18. IMAGINATION	R.	Liza throws Higgins' ____ at him
I - 19. STAGE	S.	Having lots of money
W - 20. LADY	T.	It's only ____. Low spirits and nothing else.
R - 21. SLIPPERS	U.	Liza gets her own flower ____
J - 22. FREDDY	V.	Eliza's last name
E - 23. SPEECH	W.	Gentlewoman
G - 24. HIGGINS	X.	Gives the characters a believable motivation for meeting
Y - 25. MANNERS	Y.	Social graces

Pygmalion Magic Squares 1

Match the definition with the vocabulary word. Put your answers in the magic squares below. When your answers are correct, all columns and rows will add to the same number.

A. DIGNITY
B. RESPONSIBILITY
C. PYGMALION
D. FAIR
E. PEARCE
F. SPEECH
G. ALFRED
H. FLOWERS
I. CLARA
J. SCENE
K. NEPOMMUCK
L. EYNSFORD
M. IMAGINATION
N. FREDDY
O. NATURAL
P. VULGAR

1. It's only ____. Low spirits and nothing else.
2. Higgins and Pickering both study this
3. Eliza sold these
4. I only want to be ___.
5. ____ - Hill; mother and daughter from the rainstorm in Act One
6. He created a statue of a woman so beautiful he fell in love with her
7. Liza has this; sense of personal self-worth
8. Act division
9. Guest at ambassador's reception who was fluent in many languages
10. My ____ Lady; musical version of Pygmalion
11. Alfred wanted a life free of this.
12. Tries to imitate Liza's manners
13. Eliza marries him
14. Housekeeper for Higgins
15. This Doolittle tried to blackmail Higgins.
16. Kind of language Eliza uses to tell the story of her aunt's death

A=	B=	C=	D=
E=	F=	G=	H=
I=	J=	K=	L=
M=	N=	O=	P=

Pygmalion Magic Squares 1 Answer Key

Match the definition with the vocabulary word. Put your answers in the magic squares below. When your answers are correct, all columns and rows will add to the same number.

A. DIGNITY
B. RESPONSIBILITY
C. PYGMALION
D. FAIR
E. PEARCE
F. SPEECH
G. ALFRED
H. FLOWERS
I. CLARA
J. SCENE
K. NEPOMMUCK
L. EYNSFORD
M. IMAGINATION
N. FREDDY
O. NATURAL
P. VULGAR

1. It's only ____. Low spirits and nothing else.
2. Higgins and Pickering both study this
3. Eliza sold these
4. I only want to be ___.
5. ____ - Hill; mother and daughter from the rainstorm in Act One
6. He created a statue of a woman so beautiful he fell in love with her
7. Liza has this; sense of personal self-worth
8. Act division
9. Guest at ambassador's reception who was fluent in many languages
10. My ____ Lady; musical version of Pygmalion
11. Alfred wanted a life free of this.
12. Tries to imitate Liza's manners
13. Eliza marries him
14. Housekeeper for Higgins
15. This Doolittle tried to blackmail Higgins.
16. Kind of language Eliza uses to tell the story of her aunt's death

A=7	B=11	C=6	D=10
E=14	F=2	G=15	H=3
I=12	J=8	K=9	L=5
M=1	N=13	O=4	P=16

Pygmalion Magic Squares 2

Match the definition with the vocabulary word. Put your answers in the magic squares below. When your answers are correct, all columns and rows will add to the same number.

A. DUSTBIN
B. CLARA
C. FAIR
D. NATURAL
E. FREDDY
F. LIZA
G. SHOP
H. NEPOMMUCK
I. DOOLITTLE
J. PEARCE
K. SCENE
L. PICKERING
M. DIGNITY
N. VULGAR
O. AMBASSADOR
P. ALFRED

1. He had a reception
2. I only want to be ___.
3. Housekeeper for Higgins
4. Eliza marries him
5. Eliza's last name
6. Flower girl who becomes a lady
7. This Doolittle tried to blackmail Higgins.
8. My ____ Lady; musical version of Pygmalion
9. Guest at ambassador's reception who was fluent in many languages
10. Act division
11. 'She's deliciously low--so horribly dirty....Put her in the_____'
12. Kind of language Eliza uses to tell the story of her aunt's death
13. Tries to imitate Liza's manners
14. Liza has this; sense of personal self-worth
15. Liza gets her own flower ____
16. The colonel

A=	B=	C=	D=
E=	F=	G=	H=
I=	J=	K=	L=
M=	N=	O=	P=

Pygmalion Magic Squares 2 Answer Key

Match the definition with the vocabulary word. Put your answers in the magic squares below. When your answers are correct, all columns and rows will add to the same number.

A. DUSTBIN
B. CLARA
C. FAIR
D. NATURAL
E. FREDDY
F. LIZA
G. SHOP
H. NEPOMMUCK
I. DOOLITTLE
J. PEARCE
K. SCENE
L. PICKERING
M. DIGNITY
N. VULGAR
O. AMBASSADOR
P. ALFRED

1. He had a reception
2. I only want to be ___.
3. Housekeeper for Higgins
4. Eliza marries him
5. Eliza's last name
6. Flower girl who becomes a lady
7. This Doolittle tried to blackmail Higgins.
8. My ____ Lady; musical version of Pygmalion
9. Guest at ambassador's reception who was fluent in many languages
10. Act division
11. 'She's deliciously low--so horribly dirty....Put her in the_____'
12. Kind of language Eliza uses to tell the story of her aunt's death
13. Tries to imitate Liza's manners
14. Liza has this; sense of personal self-worth
15. Liza gets her own flower ____
16. The colonel

A=11	B=13	C=8	D=2
E=4	F=6	G=15	H=9
I=5	J=3	K=10	L=16
M=14	N=12	O=1	P=7

Pygmalion Magic Squares 3

Match the definition with the vocabulary word. Put your answers in the magic squares below. When your answers are correct, all columns and rows will add to the same number.

A. FAIR
B. MANNERS
C. ACT
D. IMAGINATION
E. PYGMALION
F. HIGGINS
G. PICKERING
H. SHOP
I. AMBASSADOR
J. FREDDY
K. SPEECH
L. NEPOMMUCK
M. DOOLITTLE
N. VULGAR
O. LIZA
P. RESPONSIBILITY

1. My ____ Lady; musical version of Pygmalion
2. Kind of language Eliza uses to tell the story of her aunt's death
3. Eliza marries him
4. He created a statue of a woman so beautiful he fell in love with her
5. The colonel
6. Guest at ambassador's reception who was fluent in many languages
7. Alfred wanted a life free of this.
8. Play division
9. Flower girl who becomes a lady
10. It's only ____. Low spirits and nothing else.
11. Liza gets her own flower ____
12. Higgins and Pickering both study this
13. He had a reception
14. The professor who transforms Liza
15. Social graces
16. Eliza's last name

A=	B=	C=	D=
E=	F=	G=	H=
I=	J=	K=	L=
M=	N=	O=	P=

Pygmalion Magic Squares 3 Answer Key

Match the definition with the vocabulary word. Put your answers in the magic squares below. When your answers are correct, all columns and rows will add to the same number.

A. FAIR
B. MANNERS
C. ACT
D. IMAGINATION
E. PYGMALION
F. HIGGINS
G. PICKERING
H. SHOP
I. AMBASSADOR
J. FREDDY
K. SPEECH
L. NEPOMMUCK
M. DOOLITTLE
N. VULGAR
O. LIZA
P. RESPONSIBILITY

1. My _____ Lady; musical version of Pygmalion
2. Kind of language Eliza uses to tell the story of her aunt's death
3. Eliza marries him
4. He created a statue of a woman so beautiful he fell in love with her
5. The colonel
6. Guest at ambassador's reception who was fluent in many languages
7. Alfred wanted a life free of this.
8. Play division
9. Flower girl who becomes a lady
10. It's only _____. Low spirits and nothing else.
11. Liza gets her own flower _____
12. Higgins and Pickering both study this
13. He had a reception
14. The professor who transforms Liza
15. Social graces
16. Eliza's last name

A=1	B=15	C=8	D=10
E=4	F=14	G=5	H=11
I=13	J=3	K=12	L=6
M=16	N=2	O=9	P=7

Pygmalion Magic Squares 4

Match the definition with the vocabulary word. Put your answers in the magic squares below. When your answers are correct, all columns and rows will add to the same number.

A. HIGGINS
B. PYGMALION
C. NEPOMMUCK
D. SHAW
E. FLOWERS
F. LIZA
G. ALFRED
H. VULGAR
I. IMAGINATION
J. DIGNITY
K. AMBASSADOR
L. RAIN
M. RESPONSIBILITY
N. PEARCE
O. SPEECH
P. FAIR

1. Flower girl who becomes a lady
2. It's only ____. Low spirits and nothing else.
3. Higgins and Pickering both study this
4. Author
5. Alfred wanted a life free of this.
6. He created a statue of a woman so beautiful he fell in love with her
7. Kind of language Eliza uses to tell the story of her aunt's death
8. He had a reception
9. Guest at ambassador's reception who was fluent in many languages
10. My ____ Lady; musical version of Pygmalion
11. Liza has this; sense of personal self-worth
12. Eliza sold these
13. Gives the characters a believable motivation for meeting
14. This Doolittle tried to blackmail Higgins.
15. The professor who transforms Liza
16. Housekeeper for Higgins

A=	B=	C=	D=
E=	F=	G=	H=
I=	J=	K=	L=
M=	N=	O=	P=

Pygmalion Magic Squares 4

Match the definition with the vocabulary word. Put your answers in the magic squares below. When your answers are correct, all columns and rows will add to the same number.

A. HIGGINS
B. PYGMALION
C. NEPOMMUCK
D. SHAW
E. FLOWERS
F. LIZA
G. ALFRED
H. VULGAR
I. IMAGINATION
J. DIGNITY
K. AMBASSADOR
L. RAIN
M. RESPONSIBILITY
N. PEARCE
O. SPEECH
P. FAIR

1. Flower girl who becomes a lady
2. It's only ____. Low spirits and nothing else.
3. Higgins and Pickering both study this
4. Author
5. Alfred wanted a life free of this.
6. He created a statue of a woman so beautiful he fell in love with her
7. Kind of language Eliza uses to tell the story of her aunt's death
8. He had a reception
9. Guest at ambassador's reception who was fluent in many languages
10. My ____ Lady; musical version of Pygmalion
11. Liza has this; sense of personal self-worth
12. Eliza sold these
13. Gives the characters a believable motivation for meeting
14. This Doolittle tried to blackmail Higgins.
15. The professor who transforms Liza
16. Housekeeper for Higgins

A=15	B=6	C=9	D=4
E=12	F=1	G=14	H=7
I=2	J=11	K=8	L=13
M=5	N=16	O=3	P=10

Pygmalion Word Search 1

```
R E S P O N S I B I L I T Y B J V M Q X
T R G X P Z K X B K J Q N C F F B Q C D
A D C W Y Q J B G W X K Z K W K W V Q H
M T C L P X L N C J G K N P Y X N Y G H
B I M A G I N A T I O N B Z M L Y R D W
A M F M H C P F R K X Y F W Q K D Z K L
S P C Z S G S J K C W B F L R R L D B C
S T E G P D P N N U P X Q T O M K Q F V
A R P A D D I X M M L Z Q F R W Z V P W
D O H S R S C P S M A T S D A E E K O C
O U P G Z C K R P O D N Q C G Q Z R H H
R B D M Y S E L F P Y G M A L I O N S H
S L B V L P R R T E T F T I U A I Y N K
P E Y B P Q I C S N I S Z N V A R C I M
E X F I Z W N R F M N A R A M X A G H
E F L R A P G G Y A G C I T A A D S G G
C S X H E Q R G K S I T C U L N W Z I K
H H S S G D H K Y M D R H R F N V G H B
X D Y C Q Z D Z K H Z X G A R E L T Q K
N W D E F Z K Y L P F S X L E R Q Q J F
D C N N I B T S U D X W L F D S Q R L T
X X L E P B T M S R D O O L I T T L E T
```

Act division (5)
Alfred wanted a life free of this. (14)
Author (4)
Eliza marries him (6)
Eliza sold these (7)
Eliza's last name (9)
Flower girl who becomes a lady (4)
Gentlewoman (4)
Gives the characters a believable motivation for meeting (4)
Guest at ambassador's reception who was fluent in many languages (9)
Having lots of money (4)
He created a statue of a woman so beautiful he fell in love with her (9)
He had a reception (10)
Higgins and Pickering both study this (6)
Housekeeper for Higgins (6)
I only want to be ____. (7)
I sold flowers. I didn't sell ____. (6)
It's only ____. Low spirits and nothing else. (11)
Kind of language Eliza uses to tell the story of her aunt's death (6)
Liza gets her own flower ____ (4)
Liza has this; sense of personal self-worth (7)
Liza throws Higgins' ____ at him (8)
Making life means making ____. (7)
My ____ Lady; musical version of Pygmalion (4)
Place where play is usually performed (5)
Play division (3)
She's deliciously low--so horribly dirty....Put her in the ____. (7)
Social graces (7)
The colonel (9)
The professor who transforms Liza (7)
This Doolittle tried to blackmail Higgins. (6)
Tries to imitate Liza's manners (5)
____ - Hill; mother and daughter from the rainstorm in Act One (8)

Pygmalion Word Search 1 Answer Key

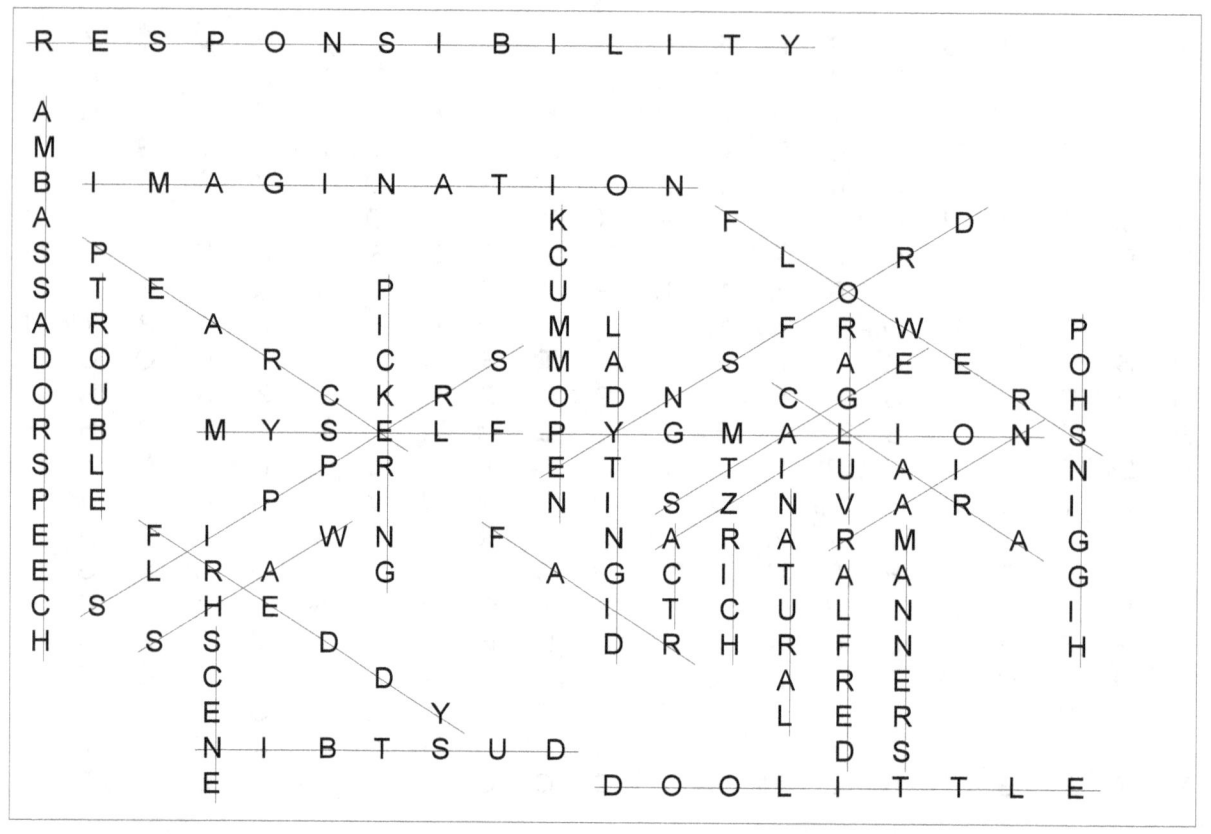

Act division (5)
Alfred wanted a life free of this. (14)
Author (4)
Eliza marries him (6)
Eliza sold these (7)
Eliza's last name (9)
Flower girl who becomes a lady (4)
Gentlewoman (4)
Gives the characters a believable motivation for meeting (4)
Guest at ambassador's reception who was fluent in many languages (9)
Having lots of money (4)
He created a statue of a woman so beautiful he fell in love with her (9)
He had a reception (10)
Higgins and Pickering both study this (6)
Housekeeper for Higgins (6)
I only want to be ____. (7)
I sold flowers. I didn't sell ___. (6)
It's only ____. Low spirits and nothing else. (11)
Kind of language Eliza uses to tell the story of her aunt's death (6)
Liza gets her own flower ____ (4)
Liza has this; sense of personal self-worth (7)
Liza throws Higgins' ____ at him (8)
Making life means making ___. (7)
My ____ Lady; musical version of Pygmalion (4)
Place where play is usually performed (5)
Play division (3)
She's deliciously low--so horribly dirty....Put her in the_____. (7)
Social graces (7)
The colonel (9)
The professor who transforms Liza (7)
This Doolittle tried to blackmail Higgins. (6)
Tries to imitate Liza's manners (5)
____ - Hill; mother and daughter from the rainstorm in Act One (8)

Pygmalion Word Search 2

```
N S L I P P E R S B E F R Y B J Q A I D
N A Z M Q R R Z Y X Y Y N P S Q B M M R
M R T F B K G D B L D H N G Y Q N B A V
D P D U V C N R R Y T R G S S Y S A G V
L H O Z R B Z W G T R V Y R F Y Y S I P
R Z O B D A V K B I G B R E G O C S N N
D T L Z G V L X W L H Q Q N Z V R A A W
N O I L A M G Y P I Y A C N R L V D T Z
T C T V T R Y P V B K L D A V Y N O I X
C M T S U W S L N I F F J M Q C H R O L
Z N L H H L N I V S P R T C M Z T E N V
K S E O N X G Z R N N E X S Q T L D N C
M C W P Y Y D A L O T D U S T B I N Y W
S Q M C O X F G R P M H X C U J T D M Y
V T H W P M S X M S C S G O S P D Y C W
B Z A S N N M Y S E L F R S V E R A I N
B H C G I S T U E R C T R C R A L R C M
S G S G E J H P C K K E S F W R N A N Q
B Z G W K R S N M K W F F C Z C J L G M
P I C K E R I N G O R Y B A E E A C T P
H B L H P R R C L C Z D K J I N F K B G
D I G N I T Y F H C Z Z J J D R E Z Z P
```

Act division (5)
Alfred wanted a life free of this. (14)
Author (4)
Eliza marries him (6)
Eliza sold these (7)
Eliza's last name (9)
Flower girl who becomes a lady (4)
Gentlewoman (4)
Gives the characters a believable motivation for meeting (4)
Guest at ambassador's reception who was fluent in many languages (9)
Having lots of money (4)
He created a statue of a woman so beautiful he fell in love with her (9)
He had a reception (10)
Higgins and Pickering both study this (6)
Housekeeper for Higgins (6)
I only want to be ____. (7)
I sold flowers. I didn't sell ____. (6)
It's only ____. Low spirits and nothing else. (11)

Kind of language Eliza uses to tell the story of her aunt's death (6)
Liza gets her own flower ____ (4)
Liza has this; sense of personal self-worth (7)
Liza throws Higgins' ____ at him (8)
Making life means making ____. (7)
My ____ Lady; musical version of Pygmalion (4)
Place where play is usually performed (5)
Play division (3)
She's deliciously low--so horribly dirty....Put her in the____. (7)
Social graces (7)
The colonel (9)
The professor who transforms Liza (7)
This Doolittle tried to blackmail Higgins. (6)
Tries to imitate Liza's manners (5)
____ - Hill; mother and daughter from the rainstorm in Act One (8)

Pygmalion Word Search 2 Answer Key

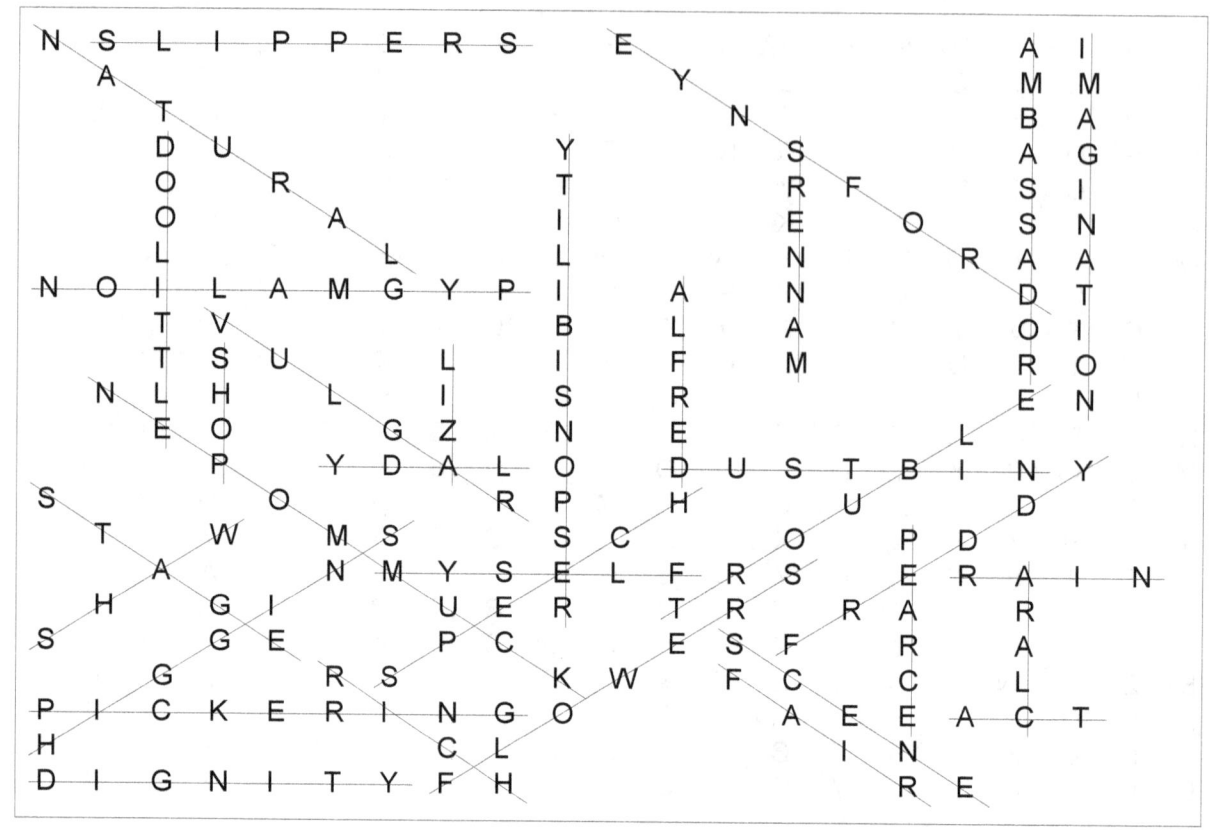

Act division (5)
Alfred wanted a life free of this. (14)
Author (4)
Eliza marries him (6)
Eliza sold these (7)
Eliza's last name (9)
Flower girl who becomes a lady (4)
Gentlewoman (4)
Gives the characters a believable motivation for meeting (4)
Guest at ambassador's reception who was fluent in many languages (9)
Having lots of money (4)
He created a statue of a woman so beautiful he fell in love with her (9)
He had a reception (10)
Higgins and Pickering both study this (6)
Housekeeper for Higgins (6)
I only want to be ___. (7)
I sold flowers. I didn't sell ___. (6)
It's only ____. Low spirits and nothing else. (11)

Kind of language Eliza uses to tell the story of her aunt's death (6)
Liza gets her own flower ____ (4)
Liza has this; sense of personal self-worth (7)
Liza throws Higgins' ____ at him (8)
Making life means making ___. (7)
My ____ Lady; musical version of Pygmalion (4)
Place where play is usually performed (5)
Play division (3)
She's deliciously low--so horribly dirty....Put her in the_____. (7)
Social graces (7)
The colonel (9)
The professor who transforms Liza (7)
This Doolittle tried to blackmail Higgins. (6)
Tries to imitate Liza's manners (5)
____ - Hill; mother and daughter from the rainstorm in Act One (8)

Pygmalion Word Search 3

```
M X Q F X M L M D U S T B I N P A M E B
S A D N H C H Y C L T C M T A B M W Y K
X K N K H Z Y S B F N A Y X T X B L N H
R R P N C H L E B P Z V C Y U V A W S F
X E N X E M Z L Q E L B U O R T S T F S
X S K E Q R R F X P P R Q Q A L S L O P
E P Q M P H S P H H K I Y Y L H A B R G
L O T H P O R Y H V D F C Z M C D F D W
T N B C S G M G D W M F R K L L O F A K
T S I L Y V H M H M R N M X E A R H N F
I I F M V G D A U K F L O W E R S Z E B
L B R F A H B L K C L V K R A A I N L N
O I F S F G H I Y N K W C G T Y E N L C
O L V L A R I O W M H K L H C C Y G Y
D I G N I T Y N P J N U G W S Y H R R X
F T Z P R A V A J V R S H L T N T I N
R Y L E V L L R C T F N O S I I A L C R
E N I A R P F F Z K I P Y D P K Z G H M
D Q B R D B R G L G P O Y W P E N A E K
D T G C V Y E S G T Q X N W E B E K R T
Y K D E H V D I J F V Z D X R P M C B W
F D C C J R H T F S G D B N S R L K H J
```

ACT	FLOWERS	NEPOMMUCK	SHOP
ALFRED	FREDDY	PEARCE	SLIPPERS
AMBASSADOR	HIGGINS	PICKERING	SPEECH
CLARA	IMAGINATION	PYGMALION	STAGE
DIGNITY	LADY	RAIN	TROUBLE
DOOLITTLE	LIZA	RESPONSIBILITY	VULGAR
DUSTBIN	MANNERS	RICH	
EYNSFORD	MYSELF	SCENE	
FAIR	NATURAL	SHAW	

Pygmalion Word Search 3 Answer Key

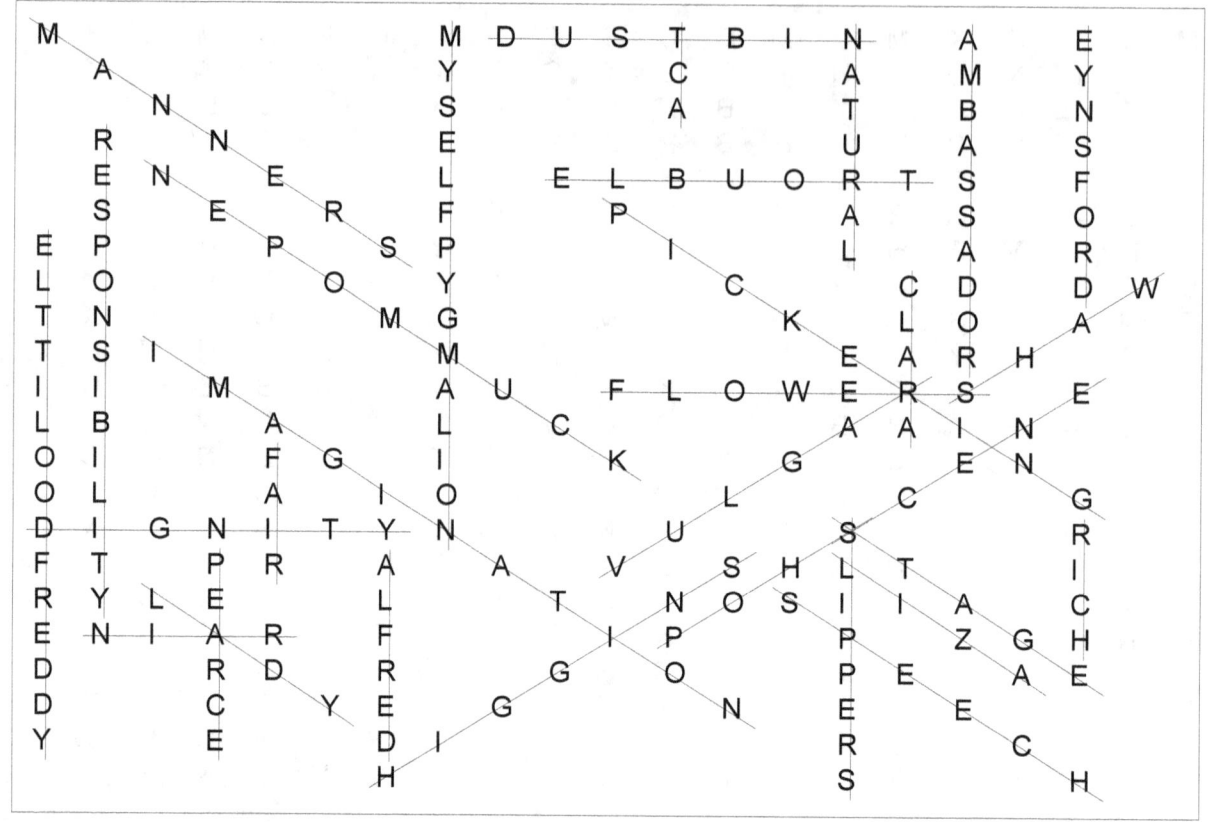

ACT	FLOWERS	NEPOMMUCK	SHOP
ALFRED	FREDDY	PEARCE	SLIPPERS
AMBASSADOR	HIGGINS	PICKERING	SPEECH
CLARA	IMAGINATION	PYGMALION	STAGE
DIGNITY	LADY	RAIN	TROUBLE
DOOLITTLE	LIZA	RESPONSIBILITY	VULGAR
DUSTBIN	MANNERS	RICH	
EYNSFORD	MYSELF	SCENE	
FAIR	NATURAL	SHAW	

Pygmalion Word Search 4

```
S D O O L I T T L E B J S S J H B T F Y
L I M A G I N A T I O N H J Z V J G A W
I Y H P T Y H J P L I Z P L Q V N J I F
P J C H P F Q D Y G B N V H H I R M R H
P Z N D L G D J G F P R X G R T W W D V
E C V E Y M W I M Z M R H E S H C R M C
R F S N J J H L A N Y M K B G N O G Y N
S Y K P N V K X L J T C Y X R F A L Z W
M Q F D B Y C X I H I Y P R S F M L Q Z
V D D R N J U N O P L J M N V W B F M W
S S F H N W M H N R I S Y D Y L A D C Q
R W V L Z F M D Y B B E W S C Z S L L Z
E H H N O L O W I F I R C N D Z S A A J
N S W W J W P X L G S E T Y G H A D R M
N A S T A G E R A I N I B T S U D Y A S
A L J K L N R X E O I C B R K O Q H S
M B T F B T J V S H P A T I D V R S C H
S T X U R A G L U V S S C Y P E A R C E
K H O R R E Z H Z Q E H W Z M Z R E P M
X R A S X A D B J S R O G Y I R E B Z H
T J T W D D L D K S H P N L L P B T W F
B B X G L H G D Y N H N G N S T P Z R S
```

ACT	FLOWERS	NEPOMMUCK	SHOP
ALFRED	FREDDY	PEARCE	SLIPPERS
AMBASSADOR	HIGGINS	PICKERING	SPEECH
CLARA	IMAGINATION	PYGMALION	STAGE
DIGNITY	LADY	RAIN	TROUBLE
DOOLITTLE	LIZA	RESPONSIBILITY	VULGAR
DUSTBIN	MANNERS	RICH	
EYNSFORD	MYSELF	SCENE	
FAIR	NATURAL	SHAW	

Pygmalion Word Search 4 Answer Key

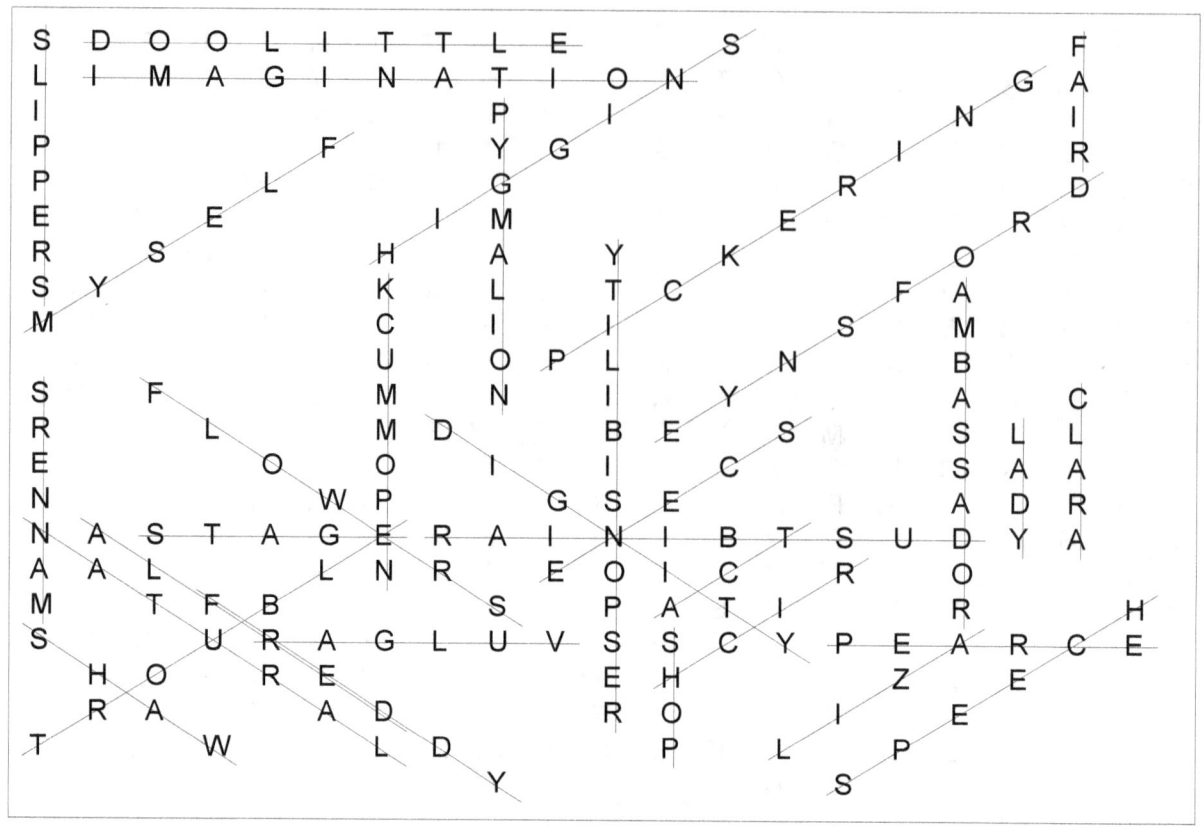

ACT	FLOWERS	NEPOMMUCK	SHOP
ALFRED	FREDDY	PEARCE	SLIPPERS
AMBASSADOR	HIGGINS	PICKERING	SPEECH
CLARA	IMAGINATION	PYGMALION	STAGE
DIGNITY	LADY	RAIN	TROUBLE
DOOLITTLE	LIZA	RESPONSIBILITY	VULGAR
DUSTBIN	MANNERS	RICH	
EYNSFORD	MYSELF	SCENE	
FAIR	NATURAL	SHAW	

Pygmalion Crossword 1

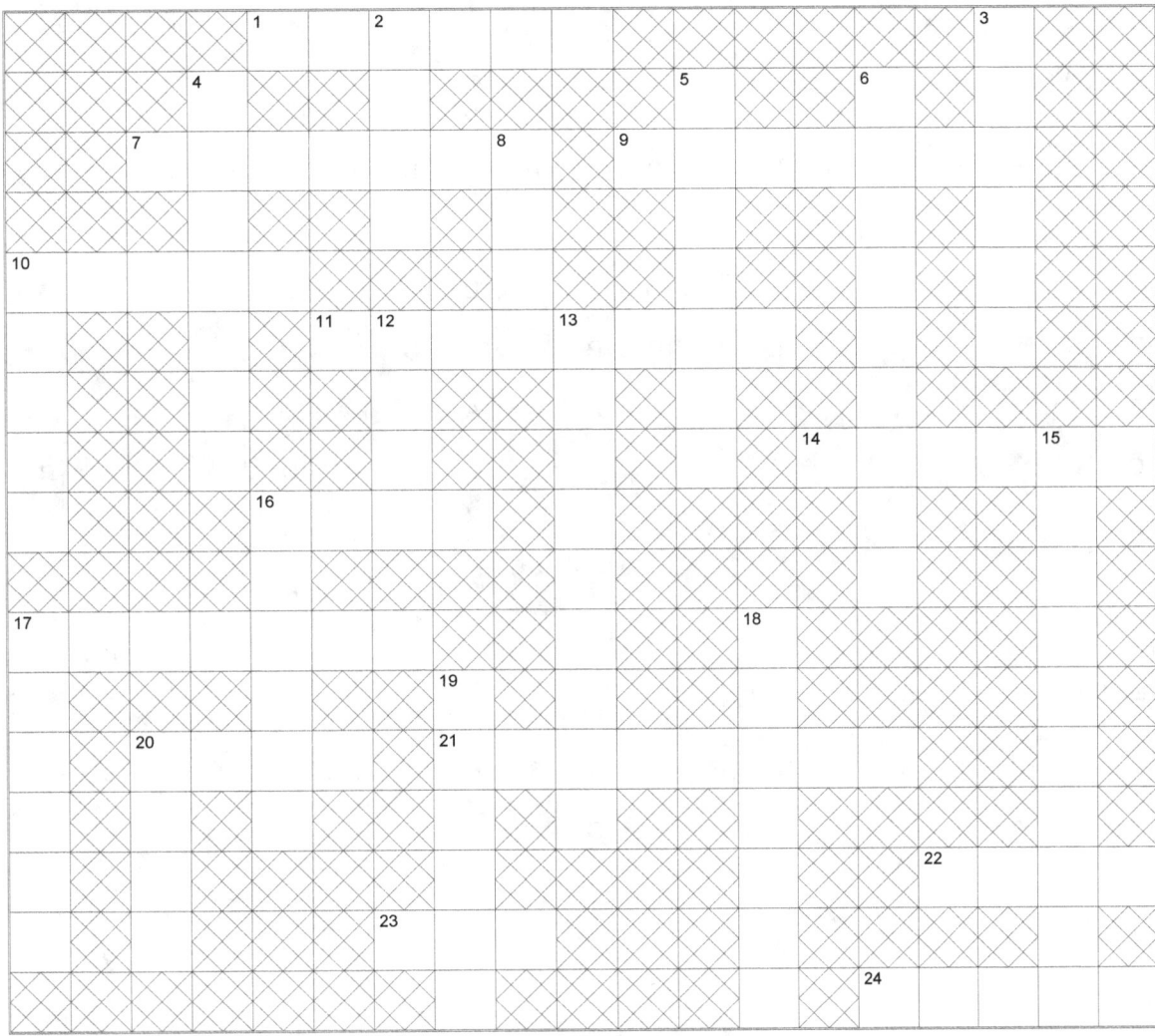

Across
1. This Doolittle tried to blackmail Higgins.
7. The professor who transforms Liza
9. Social graces
10. Act division
11. Liza throws Higgins' ____ at him
14. Kind of language Eliza uses to tell the story of her aunt's death
16. Author
17. Eliza sold these
20. Having lots of money
21. ____ - Hill; mother and daughter from the rainstorm in Act One
22. Gentlewoman
23. Play division
24. Tries to imitate Liza's manners

Down
2. My ____ Lady; musical version of Pygmalion
3. I sold flowers. I didn't sell ___.
4. Liza has this; sense of personal self-worth
5. I only want to be ___.
6. Guest at ambassador's reception who was fluent in many languages
8. Liza gets her own flower ____
10. Place where play is usually performed
12. Flower girl who becomes a lady
13. The colonel
15. He had a reception
16. Higgins and Pickering both study this
17. Eliza marries him
18. Making life means making ___.
19. Housekeeper for Higgins
20. Gives the characters a believable motivation for meeting

Pygmalion Crossword 1 Answer Key

Across
1. This Doolittle tried to blackmail Higgins.
7. The professor who transforms Liza
9. Social graces
10. Act division
11. Liza throws Higgins' ____ at him
14. Kind of language Eliza uses to tell the story of her aunt's death
16. Author
17. Eliza sold these
20. Having lots of money
21. ____ - Hill; mother and daughter from the rainstorm in Act One
22. Gentlewoman
23. Play division
24. Tries to imitate Liza's manners

Down
2. My ____ Lady; musical version of Pygmalion
3. I sold flowers. I didn't sell ___.
4. Liza has this; sense of personal self-worth
5. I only want to be ___.
6. Guest at ambassador's reception who was fluent in many languages
8. Liza gets her own flower ____
10. Place where play is usually performed
12. Flower girl who becomes a lady
13. The colonel
15. He had a reception
16. Higgins and Pickering both study this
17. Eliza marries him
18. Making life means making ___.
19. Housekeeper for Higgins
20. Gives the characters a believable motivation for meeting

Pygmalion Crossword 2

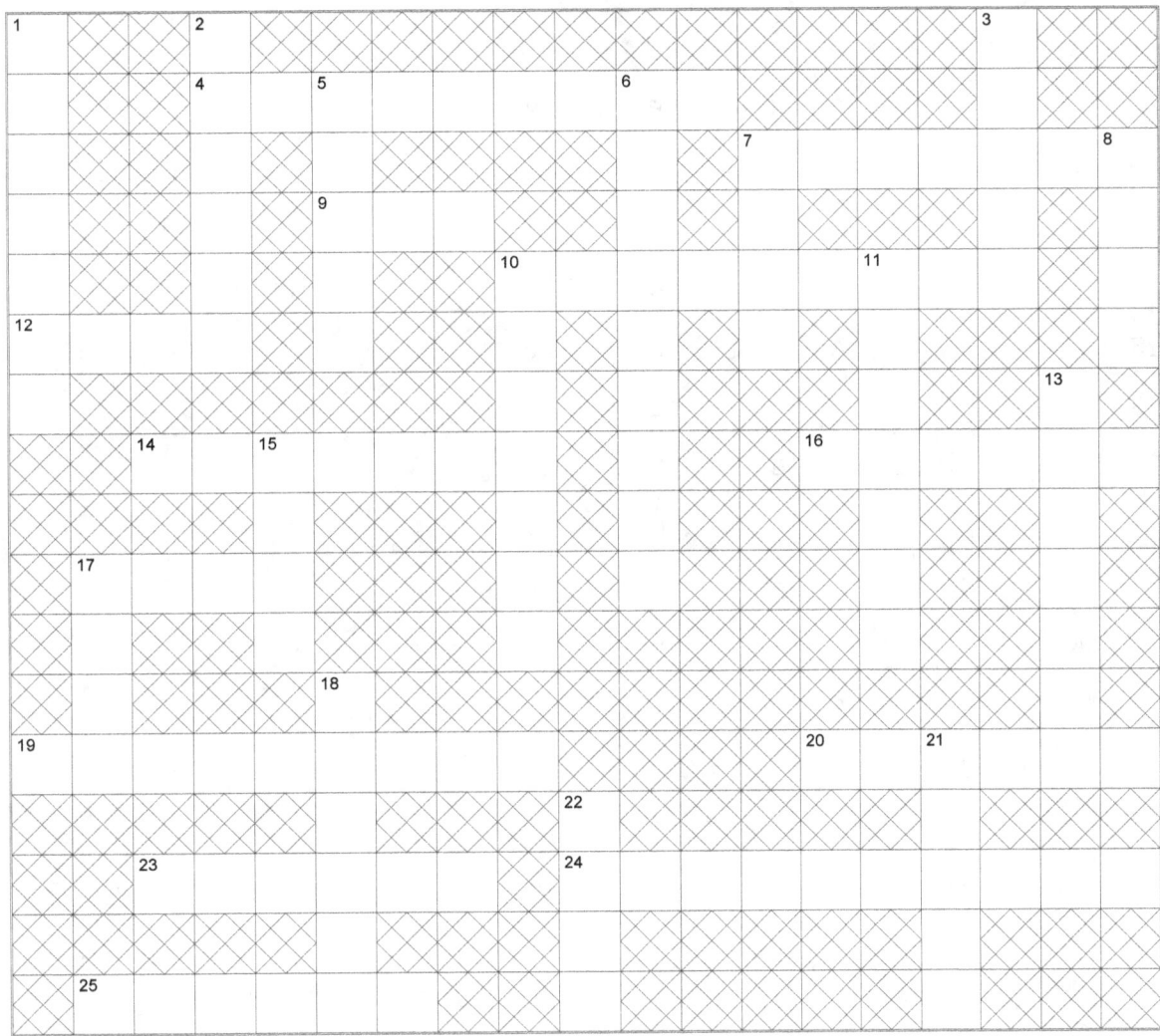

Across
4. The colonel
7. Eliza sold these
9. Play division
10. Eliza's last name
12. Having lots of money
14. She's deliciously low--so horribly dirty....Put her in the_____.
16. Kind of language Eliza uses to tell the story of her aunt's death
17. Flower girl who becomes a lady
19. He created a statue of a woman so beautiful he fell in love with her
20. I sold flowers. I didn't sell ___.
23. Housekeeper for Higgins
24. He had a reception
25. Eliza marries him

Down
1. Social graces
2. Higgins and Pickering both study this
3. Act division
5. Tries to imitate Liza's manners
6. Guest at ambassador's reception who was fluent in many languages
7. My ____ Lady; musical version of Pygmalion
8. Liza gets her own flower ____
10. Liza has this; sense of personal self-worth
11. Making life means making ___.
13. I only want to be ___.
15. Author
17. Gentlewoman
18. This Doolittle tried to blackmail Higgins.
21. Place where play is usually performed
22. Gives the characters a believable motivation for meeting

Pygmalion Crossword 2 Answer Key

	1 M		2 S										3 S	
	A		4 P	5 I	C	K	E	R	6 I	N	G		C	
	N		E						E	7 F	L	O	W	8 S
	N		E	9 A	C	T			P	A			N	H
	E		C	R			10 D	O	O	L	11 T	T	L	O
12 R	I	C	H	A			I		M	R	R			P
S							G		M		O		13 N	
		14 D	15 U	S	T	B	I	N		16 V	U	L	G	A R
			H				I		C		B		T	
		17 L	I	Z	A		T		K		L		U	
		A		W			Y				E		R	
		D			18 A								A	
19 P	Y	G	M	A	L	I	O	N		20 M	Y	21 S	E	L F
					F				22 R			T		
		23 P	E	A	R	C	E		24 A	M	B	A	S S A D O R
					E				I			G		
		25 F	R	E	D	D	Y		N			E		

Across
- 4. The colonel
- 7. Eliza sold these
- 9. Play division
- 10. Eliza's last name
- 12. Having lots of money
- 14. She's deliciously low--so horribly dirty....Put her in the_____.
- 16. Kind of language Eliza uses to tell the story of her aunt's death
- 17. Flower girl who becomes a lady
- 19. He created a statue of a woman so beautiful he fell in love with her
- 20. I sold flowers. I didn't sell ___.
- 23. Housekeeper for Higgins
- 24. He had a reception
- 25. Eliza marries him

Down
- 1. Social graces
- 2. Higgins and Pickering both study this
- 3. Act division
- 5. Tries to imitate Liza's manners
- 6. Guest at ambassador's reception who was fluent in many languages
- 7. My ____ Lady; musical version of Pygmalion
- 8. Liza gets her own flower ____
- 10. Liza has this; sense of personal self-worth
- 11. Making life means making ___.
- 13. I only want to be ___.
- 15. Author
- 17. Gentlewoman
- 18. This Doolittle tried to blackmail Higgins.
- 21. Place where play is usually performed
- 22. Gives the characters a believable motivation for meeting

Pygmalion Crossword 3

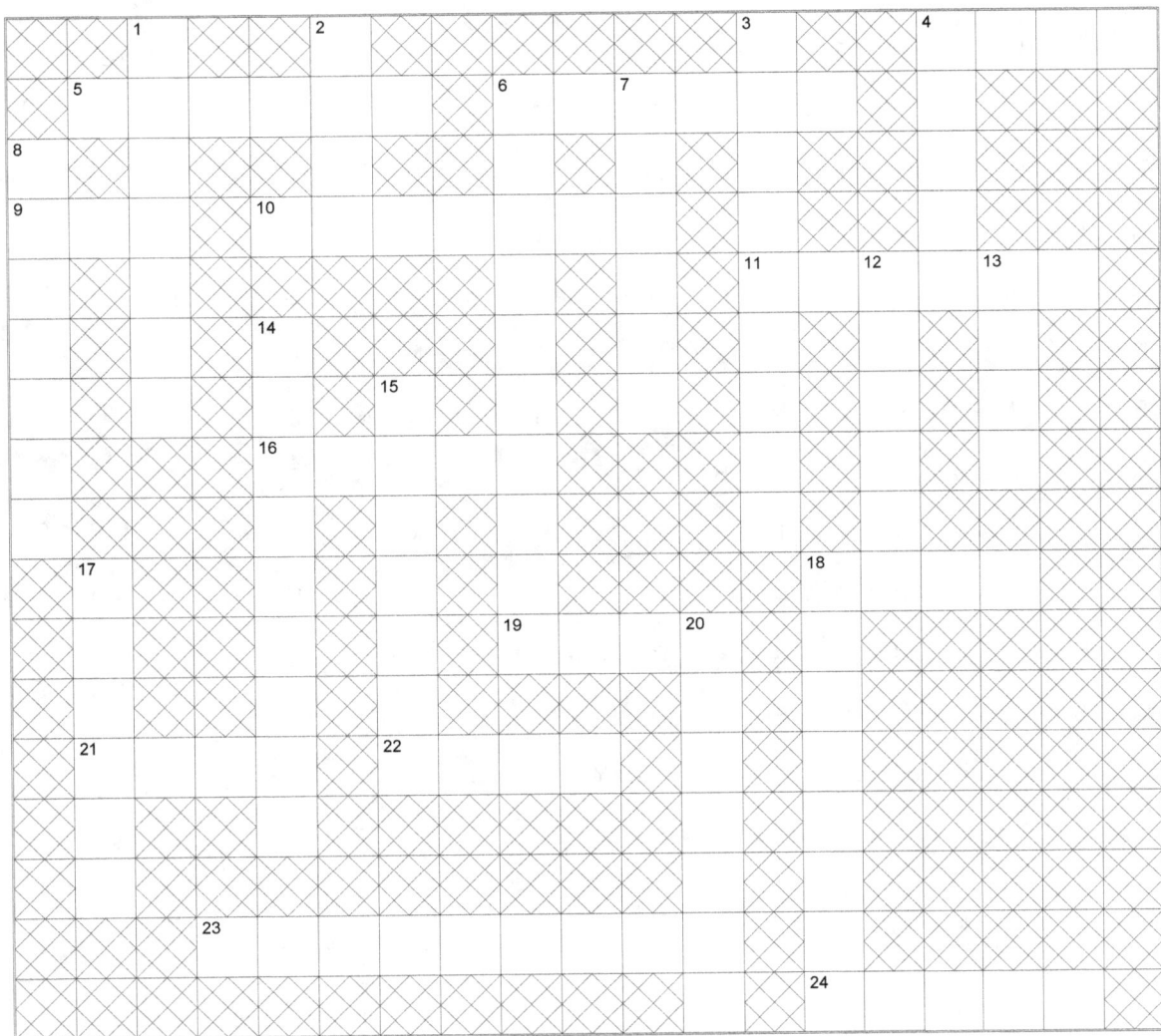

Across
4. Liza gets her own flower ____
5. Kind of language Eliza uses to tell the story of her aunt's death
6. This Doolittle tried to blackmail Higgins.
9. Play division
10. Making life means making ___.
11. I sold flowers. I didn't sell ___.
16. Tries to imitate Liza's manners
18. Author
19. Having lots of money
21. Gives the characters a believable motivation for meeting
22. Gentlewoman
23. He created a statue of a woman so beautiful he fell in love with her
24. Place where play is usually performed

Down
1. She's deliciously low--so horribly dirty....Put her in the_____.
2. My ____ Lady; musical version of Pygmalion
3. Guest at ambassador's reception who was fluent in many languages
4. Act division
6. He had a reception
7. Eliza marries him
8. Social graces
12. Higgins and Pickering both study this
13. Flower girl who becomes a lady
14. The colonel
15. I only want to be ___.
17. Housekeeper for Higgins
18. Liza throws Higgins' ____ at him
20. The professor who transforms Liza

Pygmalion Crossword 3 Answer Key

		1 D			2 F				3 N		4 S	H	O	P
	5	V	U	L	G	A	R	6 A	L	7 F	R	E	D		C	
8 M		S				I		M		R		P			E	
9 A	10 C	T	R	O	U	B	L	E		O		11 M	12 Y	13 S	E	L	F
N		B						A		D		M		P		I	
N		I		14 P				S		D				E		Z	
E		N		I			15 N	S		Y		U		E		A	
R			16 C	L	A	R	A					C		E			
S			K			T		D				K		C			
		17 P		E		U		O				18 S	H	A	W		
		E		R		R		19 R	I	20 C	H			L			
		A		I		A				I				I			
	21 R	A	I	N		22 L	A	D	Y		G		P			
		C		G						G		P			
		E								I		E			
				23 P	Y	G	M	A	L	I	O	N	R		
										S	24 S	T	A	G	E

Across
4. Liza gets her own flower ____
5. Kind of language Eliza uses to tell the story of her aunt's death
6. This Doolittle tried to blackmail Higgins.
9. Play division
10. Making life means making ___.
11. I sold flowers. I didn't sell ___.
16. Tries to imitate Liza's manners
18. Author
19. Having lots of money
21. Gives the characters a believable motivation for meeting
22. Gentlewoman
23. He created a statue of a woman so beautiful he fell in love with her
24. Place where play is usually performed

Down
1. She's deliciously low--so horribly dirty....Put her in the_____.
2. My ____ Lady; musical version of Pygmalion
3. Guest at ambassador's reception who was fluent in many languages
4. Act division
6. He had a reception
7. Eliza marries him
8. Social graces
12. Higgins and Pickering both study this
13. Flower girl who becomes a lady
14. The colonel
15. I only want to be ___.
17. Housekeeper for Higgins
18. Liza throws Higgins' ____ at him
20. The professor who transforms Liza

Pygmalion Crossword 4

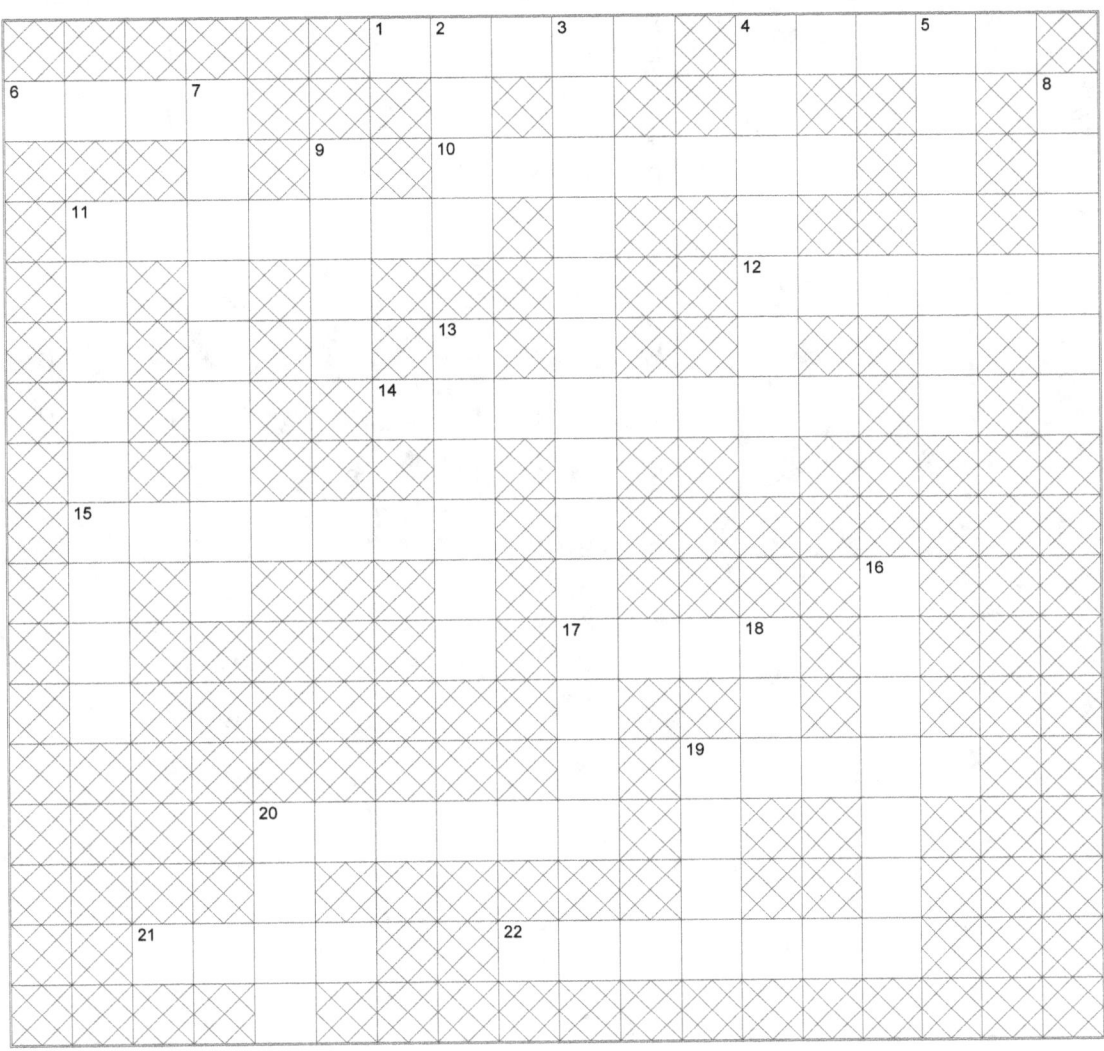

Across
1. Tries to imitate Liza's manners
4. Act division
6. Liza gets her own flower ____
10. She's deliciously low--so horribly dirty....Put her in the_____.
11. Liza has this; sense of personal self-worth
12. Housekeeper for Higgins
14. ____ - Hill; mother and daughter from the rainstorm in Act One
15. Making life means making ___.
17. Flower girl who becomes a lady
19. Place where play is usually performed
20. Eliza marries him
21. Gives the characters a believable motivation for meeting
22. Eliza sold these

Down
2. Gentlewoman
3. Alfred wanted a life free of this.
4. Liza throws Higgins' ____ at him
5. I only want to be ___.
7. He created a statue of a woman so beautiful he fell in love with her
8. Higgins and Pickering both study this
9. Having lots of money
11. Eliza's last name
13. I sold flowers. I didn't sell ___.
16. The professor who transforms Liza
18. Play division
19. Author
20. My ____ Lady; musical version of Pygmalion

Pygmalion Crossword 4 Answer Key

Across
1. Tries to imitate Liza's manners
4. Act division
6. Liza gets her own flower ____
10. She's deliciously low--so horribly dirty....Put her in the _____.
11. Liza has this; sense of personal self-worth
12. Housekeeper for Higgins
14. ____ - Hill; mother and daughter from the rainstorm in Act One
15. Making life means making ___.
17. Flower girl who becomes a lady
19. Place where play is usually performed
20. Eliza marries him
21. Gives the characters a believable motivation for meeting
22. Eliza sold these

Down
2. Gentlewoman
3. Alfred wanted a life free of this.
4. Liza throws Higgins' ____ at him
5. I only want to be ___.
7. He created a statue of a woman so beautiful he fell in love with her
8. Higgins and Pickering both study this
9. Having lots of money
11. Eliza's last name
13. I sold flowers. I didn't sell ___.
16. The professor who transforms Liza
18. Play division
19. Author
20. My ____ Lady; musical version of Pygmalion

Pygmalion

RICH	ACT	CLARA	MANNERS	SPEECH
LADY	PICKERING	TROUBLE	NATURAL	FAIR
EYNSFORD	AMBASSADOR	FREE SPACE	VULGAR	LIZA
SHAW	PYGMALION	NEPOMMUCK	SHOP	DUSTBIN
DIGNITY	MYSELF	ALFRED	IMAGINATION	STAGE

Pygmalion

DOOLITTLE	RESPONSIBILITY	FLOWERS	FREDDY	SCENE
HIGGINS	RAIN	PEARCE	STAGE	IMAGINATION
ALFRED	MYSELF	FREE SPACE	DUSTBIN	SHOP
NEPOMMUCK	PYGMALION	SHAW	LIZA	VULGAR
SLIPPERS	AMBASSADOR	EYNSFORD	FAIR	NATURAL

Pygmalion

SLIPPERS	SHAW	TROUBLE	NEPOMMUCK	LIZA
VULGAR	SCENE	RICH	RESPONSIBILITY	FLOWERS
NATURAL	PICKERING	FREE SPACE	AMBASSADOR	CLARA
LADY	MANNERS	DOOLITTLE	ACT	FREDDY
PYGMALION	STAGE	RAIN	SPEECH	FAIR

Pygmalion

DUSTBIN	MYSELF	SHOP	IMAGINATION	DIGNITY
EYNSFORD	PEARCE	HIGGINS	FAIR	SPEECH
RAIN	STAGE	FREE SPACE	FREDDY	ACT
DOOLITTLE	MANNERS	LADY	CLARA	AMBASSADOR
ALFRED	PICKERING	NATURAL	FLOWERS	RESPONSIBILITY

Pygmalion

STAGE	LIZA	HIGGINS	RESPONSIBILITY	SCENE
AMBASSADOR	LADY	TROUBLE	FLOWERS	NATURAL
SLIPPERS	MANNERS	FREE SPACE	RICH	IMAGINATION
DUSTBIN	DIGNITY	ALFRED	FAIR	FREDDY
SHAW	ACT	PICKERING	DOOLITTLE	PEARCE

Pygmalion

CLARA	MYSELF	EYNSFORD	SHOP	VULGAR
SPEECH	RAIN	PYGMALION	PEARCE	DOOLITTLE
PICKERING	ACT	FREE SPACE	FREDDY	FAIR
ALFRED	DIGNITY	DUSTBIN	IMAGINATION	RICH
NEPOMMUCK	MANNERS	SLIPPERS	NATURAL	FLOWERS

Pygmalion

MYSELF	SHOP	PEARCE	RAIN	IMAGINATION
VULGAR	FREDDY	LIZA	CLARA	DIGNITY
FLOWERS	PYGMALION	FREE SPACE	NEPOMMUCK	FAIR
SHAW	DOOLITTLE	ALFRED	NATURAL	DUSTBIN
PICKERING	RICH	TROUBLE	EYNSFORD	RESPONSIBILITY

Pygmalion

SPEECH	AMBASSADOR	STAGE	LADY	ACT
SLIPPERS	MANNERS	HIGGINS	RESPONSIBILITY	EYNSFORD
TROUBLE	RICH	FREE SPACE	DUSTBIN	NATURAL
ALFRED	DOOLITTLE	SHAW	FAIR	NEPOMMUCK
SCENE	PYGMALION	FLOWERS	DIGNITY	CLARA

Pygmalion

RESPONSIBILITY	MYSELF	FAIR	VULGAR	SPEECH
MANNERS	RICH	IMAGINATION	HIGGINS	AMBASSADOR
DOOLITTLE	STAGE	FREE SPACE	FREDDY	NEPOMMUCK
DIGNITY	SLIPPERS	TROUBLE	PYGMALION	RAIN
ACT	ALFRED	PICKERING	LADY	CLARA

Pygmalion

FLOWERS	SHAW	PEARCE	SHOP	SCENE
LIZA	NATURAL	EYNSFORD	CLARA	LADY
PICKERING	ALFRED	FREE SPACE	RAIN	PYGMALION
TROUBLE	SLIPPERS	DIGNITY	NEPOMMUCK	FREDDY
DUSTBIN	STAGE	DOOLITTLE	AMBASSADOR	HIGGINS

Pygmalion

SCENE	CLARA	FAIR	LIZA	TROUBLE
ACT	IMAGINATION	RAIN	PYGMALION	STAGE
HIGGINS	DIGNITY	FREE SPACE	SHOP	PEARCE
ALFRED	DOOLITTLE	FREDDY	LADY	EYNSFORD
SPEECH	VULGAR	MANNERS	FLOWERS	AMBASSADOR

Pygmalion

PICKERING	SHAW	NEPOMMUCK	SLIPPERS	NATURAL
MYSELF	DUSTBIN	RICH	AMBASSADOR	FLOWERS
MANNERS	VULGAR	FREE SPACE	EYNSFORD	LADY
FREDDY	DOOLITTLE	ALFRED	PEARCE	SHOP
RESPONSIBILITY	DIGNITY	HIGGINS	STAGE	PYGMALION

Pygmalion

PYGMALION	LIZA	CLARA	EYNSFORD	NATURAL
SLIPPERS	PICKERING	ACT	FREDDY	ALFRED
DIGNITY	SCENE	FREE SPACE	AMBASSADOR	IMAGINATION
DOOLITTLE	MANNERS	PEARCE	SPEECH	FAIR
LADY	DUSTBIN	MYSELF	SHAW	SHOP

Pygmalion

VULGAR	TROUBLE	RICH	NEPOMMUCK	HIGGINS
RAIN	FLOWERS	RESPONSIBILITY	SHOP	SHAW
MYSELF	DUSTBIN	FREE SPACE	FAIR	SPEECH
PEARCE	MANNERS	DOOLITTLE	IMAGINATION	AMBASSADOR
STAGE	SCENE	DIGNITY	ALFRED	FREDDY

Pygmalion

SLIPPERS	RAIN	TROUBLE	MYSELF	NATURAL
SHAW	MANNERS	FLOWERS	CLARA	NEPOMMUCK
LIZA	RESPONSIBILITY	FREE SPACE	FAIR	SCENE
SPEECH	PEARCE	ALFRED	VULGAR	RICH
DIGNITY	HIGGINS	DOOLITTLE	AMBASSADOR	EYNSFORD

Pygmalion

LADY	PICKERING	SHOP	FREDDY	DUSTBIN
IMAGINATION	ACT	PYGMALION	EYNSFORD	AMBASSADOR
DOOLITTLE	HIGGINS	FREE SPACE	RICH	VULGAR
ALFRED	PEARCE	SPEECH	SCENE	FAIR
STAGE	RESPONSIBILITY	LIZA	NEPOMMUCK	CLARA

Pygmalion

PICKERING	SPEECH	EYNSFORD	DIGNITY	MYSELF
LADY	NATURAL	DOOLITTLE	SCENE	ACT
AMBASSADOR	NEPOMMUCK	FREE SPACE	STAGE	PEARCE
RICH	SHAW	ALFRED	CLARA	FLOWERS
LIZA	MANNERS	RESPONSIBILITY	PYGMALION	TROUBLE

Pygmalion

HIGGINS	FAIR	SHOP	DUSTBIN	SLIPPERS
IMAGINATION	VULGAR	RAIN	TROUBLE	PYGMALION
RESPONSIBILITY	MANNERS	FREE SPACE	FLOWERS	CLARA
ALFRED	SHAW	RICH	PEARCE	STAGE
FREDDY	NEPOMMUCK	AMBASSADOR	ACT	SCENE

Pygmalion

VULGAR	SLIPPERS	FAIR	ALFRED	DIGNITY
PICKERING	SPEECH	NATURAL	FLOWERS	SHAW
PEARCE	TROUBLE	FREE SPACE	LADY	HIGGINS
FREDDY	DUSTBIN	RESPONSIBILITY	ACT	DOOLITTLE
NEPOMMUCK	EYNSFORD	LIZA	PYGMALION	SHOP

Pygmalion

STAGE	SCENE	MANNERS	CLARA	RICH
RAIN	MYSELF	AMBASSADOR	SHOP	PYGMALION
LIZA	EYNSFORD	FREE SPACE	DOOLITTLE	ACT
RESPONSIBILITY	DUSTBIN	FREDDY	HIGGINS	LADY
IMAGINATION	TROUBLE	PEARCE	SHAW	FLOWERS

Pygmalion

LIZA	SLIPPERS	AMBASSADOR	MANNERS	FAIR
SHAW	FLOWERS	EYNSFORD	ALFRED	RAIN
RICH	FREDDY	FREE SPACE	ACT	CLARA
PYGMALION	MYSELF	SHOP	VULGAR	DIGNITY
SCENE	STAGE	NEPOMMUCK	TROUBLE	DOOLITTLE

Pygmalion

PICKERING	IMAGINATION	HIGGINS	LADY	NATURAL
DUSTBIN	PEARCE	SPEECH	DOOLITTLE	TROUBLE
NEPOMMUCK	STAGE	FREE SPACE	DIGNITY	VULGAR
SHOP	MYSELF	PYGMALION	CLARA	ACT
RESPONSIBILITY	FREDDY	RICH	RAIN	ALFRED

Pygmalion

AMBASSADOR	RESPONSIBILITY	MANNERS	RAIN	NATURAL
VULGAR	IMAGINATION	DIGNITY	MYSELF	HIGGINS
LIZA	FREDDY	FREE SPACE	ACT	PYGMALION
EYNSFORD	PEARCE	SCENE	SLIPPERS	NEPOMMUCK
FLOWERS	DOOLITTLE	CLARA	STAGE	LADY

Pygmalion

FAIR	SPEECH	TROUBLE	SHAW	DUSTBIN
PICKERING	ALFRED	RICH	LADY	STAGE
CLARA	DOOLITTLE	FREE SPACE	NEPOMMUCK	SLIPPERS
SCENE	PEARCE	EYNSFORD	PYGMALION	ACT
SHOP	FREDDY	LIZA	HIGGINS	MYSELF

Pygmalion

ACT	PEARCE	CLARA	SLIPPERS	ALFRED
VULGAR	MYSELF	SHOP	SHAW	AMBASSADOR
SPEECH	IMAGINATION	FREE SPACE	PICKERING	LADY
FREDDY	RICH	NEPOMMUCK	DIGNITY	EYNSFORD
HIGGINS	RESPONSIBILITY	RAIN	NATURAL	TROUBLE

Pygmalion

DOOLITTLE	PYGMALION	FLOWERS	STAGE	MANNERS
SCENE	LIZA	FAIR	TROUBLE	NATURAL
RAIN	RESPONSIBILITY	FREE SPACE	EYNSFORD	DIGNITY
NEPOMMUCK	RICH	FREDDY	LADY	PICKERING
DUSTBIN	IMAGINATION	SPEECH	AMBASSADOR	SHAW

Pygmalion

RESPONSIBILITY	EYNSFORD	PYGMALION	LIZA	AMBASSADOR
MANNERS	SLIPPERS	VULGAR	FLOWERS	DUSTBIN
LADY	ACT	FREE SPACE	TROUBLE	HIGGINS
NEPOMMUCK	PEARCE	NATURAL	SPEECH	RAIN
SHAW	ALFRED	SHOP	RICH	MYSELF

Pygmalion

STAGE	FREDDY	SCENE	CLARA	FAIR
IMAGINATION	DOOLITTLE	PICKERING	MYSELF	RICH
SHOP	ALFRED	FREE SPACE	RAIN	SPEECH
NATURAL	PEARCE	NEPOMMUCK	HIGGINS	TROUBLE
DIGNITY	ACT	LADY	DUSTBIN	FLOWERS

Pygmalion

LADY	DOOLITTLE	MYSELF	VULGAR	PICKERING
SLIPPERS	TROUBLE	HIGGINS	SCENE	RAIN
CLARA	ACT	FREE SPACE	FAIR	NATURAL
NEPOMMUCK	STAGE	FREDDY	MANNERS	DUSTBIN
IMAGINATION	PYGMALION	EYNSFORD	ALFRED	RESPONSIBILITY

Pygmalion

PEARCE	FLOWERS	LIZA	SPEECH	SHOP
RICH	AMBASSADOR	SHAW	RESPONSIBILITY	ALFRED
EYNSFORD	PYGMALION	FREE SPACE	DUSTBIN	MANNERS
FREDDY	STAGE	NEPOMMUCK	NATURAL	FAIR
DIGNITY	ACT	CLARA	RAIN	SCENE

Pygmalion

ACT	SHOP	LIZA	FLOWERS	NEPOMMUCK
VULGAR	IMAGINATION	SCENE	SLIPPERS	PEARCE
CLARA	FAIR	FREE SPACE	NATURAL	EYNSFORD
FREDDY	DOOLITTLE	SHAW	RAIN	MYSELF
TROUBLE	RESPONSIBILITY	RICH	SPEECH	DUSTBIN

Pygmalion

PYGMALION	HIGGINS	LADY	MANNERS	DIGNITY
ALFRED	STAGE	PICKERING	DUSTBIN	SPEECH
RICH	RESPONSIBILITY	FREE SPACE	MYSELF	RAIN
SHAW	DOOLITTLE	FREDDY	EYNSFORD	NATURAL
AMBASSADOR	FAIR	CLARA	PEARCE	SLIPPERS

Pygmalion Word List

No.	Word	Clue/Definition
1.	AMIABLE	Friendly and agreeable
2.	ASUNDER	Apart from each other in position or direction
3.	BILIOUS	Appearing as if experiencing gastric distress caused by a disorder of the liver
4.	BROUGHAM	A closed four-wheeled carriage with an open driver's seat in front
5.	CONDESCENSION	To descend to the level of one considered inferior
6.	DEMEAN	To humble oneself
7.	DEPRECIATING	Belittling
8.	DOGMATICALLY	Characterized by an authoritative, arrogant assertion of unproved or unprovable principles
9.	FROWZY	Sloppy; slovenly
10.	GUMPTION	Boldness or enterprise; initiative or aggressiveness
11.	IMPETUOUS	Impulsive and passionate
12.	INCORRIGIBLE	Incapable of being corrected or reformed
13.	MAGNANIMOUS	Courageously noble
14.	MENDACITY	Begging
15.	MISCELLANEOUS	Having a variety of characteristics, abilities, or appearances
16.	PEDANTIC	By the book; following the rules exactly
17.	PEREMPTORILY	Not allowing contradiction or refusal; commanding
18.	PLINTH	A block or slab on which a pedestal, column or statue is placed
19.	PRODIGAL	Rashly or wastefully extravagant
20.	PURGATORY	A place or condition of suffering, expiation or remorse
21.	REMONSTRANCE	An expression of protest, complaint or reproof
22.	REPUDIATES	Rejects the validity or authority of
23.	SOMNAMBULIST	Sleepwalker
24.	TOGS	Clothes
25.	ZEPHYR	Something that is airy, insubstantial or passing

Copyrighted

Pygmalion Vocabulary Fill In The Blanks 1

_____ 1. Sleepwalker

_____ 2. Impulsive and passionate

_____ 3. Clothes

_____ 4. A place or condition of suffering, expiation or remorse

_____ 5. Boldness or enterprise; initiative or aggressiveness

_____ 6. A closed four-wheeled carriage with an open driver's seat in front

_____ 7. Courageously noble

_____ 8. To humble oneself

_____ 9. Characterized by an authoritative, arrogant assertion of unproved or unprovable principles

_____ 10. To descend to the level of one considered inferior

_____ 11. Appearing as if experiencing gastric distress caused by a disorder of the liver

_____ 12. Apart from each other in position or direction

_____ 13. Sloppy; slovenly

_____ 14. Rejects the validity or authority of

_____ 15. Incapable of being corrected or reformed

_____ 16. Begging

_____ 17. Friendly and agreeable

_____ 18. Not allowing contradiction or refusal; commanding

_____ 19. Something that is airy, insubstantial or passing

_____ 20. An expression of protest, complaint or reproof

Pygmalion Vocabulary Fill In The Blanks 1 Answer Key

SOMNAMBULIST	1. Sleepwalker
IMPETUOUS	2. Impulsive and passionate
TOGS	3. Clothes
PURGATORY	4. A place or condition of suffering, expiation or remorse
GUMPTION	5. Boldness or enterprise; initiative or aggressiveness
BROUGHAM	6. A closed four-wheeled carriage with an open driver's seat in front
MAGNANIMOUS	7. Courageously noble
DEMEAN	8. To humble oneself
DOGMATICALLY	9. Characterized by an authoritative, arrogant assertion of unproved or unprovable principles
CONDESCENSION	10. To descend to the level of one considered inferior
BILIOUS	11. Appearing as if experiencing gastric distress caused by a disorder of the liver
ASUNDER	12. Apart from each other in position or direction
FROWZY	13. Sloppy; slovenly
REPUDIATES	14. Rejects the validity or authority of
INCORRIGIBLE	15. Incapable of being corrected or reformed
MENDACITY	16. Begging
AMIABLE	17. Friendly and agreeable
PEREMPTORILY	18. Not allowing contradiction or refusal; commanding
ZEPHYR	19. Something that is airy, insubstantial or passing
REMONSTRANCE	20. An expression of protest, complaint or reproof

Pygmalion Vocabulary Fill In The Blanks 2

_____ 1. Impulsive and passionate

_____ 2. Appearing as if experiencing gastric distress caused by a disorder of the liver

_____ 3. An expression of protest, complaint or reproof

_____ 4. Boldness or enterprise; initiative or aggressiveness

_____ 5. Apart from each other in position or direction

_____ 6. By the book; following the rules exactly

_____ 7. A place or condition of suffering, expiation or remorse

_____ 8. Begging

_____ 9. To humble oneself

_____ 10. Something that is airy, insubstantial or passing

_____ 11. Belittling

_____ 12. Rejects the validity or authority of

_____ 13. Courageously noble

_____ 14. Sloppy; slovenly

_____ 15. Not allowing contradiction or refusal; commanding

_____ 16. Friendly and agreeable

_____ 17. A closed four-wheeled carriage with an open driver's seat in front

_____ 18. Clothes

_____ 19. Having a variety of characteristics, abilities, or appearances

_____ 20. Incapable of being corrected or reformed

Pygmalion Vocabulary Fill In The Blanks 2 Answer Key

IMPETUOUS	1. Impulsive and passionate
BILIOUS	2. Appearing as if experiencing gastric distress caused by a disorder of the liver
REMONSTRANCE	3. An expression of protest, complaint or reproof
GUMPTION	4. Boldness or enterprise; initiative or aggressiveness
ASUNDER	5. Apart from each other in position or direction
PEDANTIC	6. By the book; following the rules exactly
PURGATORY	7. A place or condition of suffering, expiation or remorse
MENDACITY	8. Begging
DEMEAN	9. To humble oneself
ZEPHYR	10. Something that is airy, insubstantial or passing
DEPRECIATING	11. Belittling
REPUDIATES	12. Rejects the validity or authority of
MAGNANIMOUS	13. Courageously noble
FROWZY	14. Sloppy; slovenly
PEREMPTORILY	15. Not allowing contradiction or refusal; commanding
AMIABLE	16. Friendly and agreeable
BROUGHAM	17. A closed four-wheeled carriage with an open driver's seat in front
TOGS	18. Clothes
MISCELLANEOUS	19. Having a variety of characteristics, abilities, or appearances
INCORRIGIBLE	20. Incapable of being corrected or reformed

Pygmalion Vocabulary Fill In The Blanks 3

_____ 1. Apart from each other in position or direction

_____ 2. Friendly and agreeable

_____ 3. Characterized by an authoritative, arrogant assertion of unproved or unprovable principles

_____ 4. Appearing as if experiencing gastric distress caused by a disorder of the liver

_____ 5. An expression of protest, complaint or reproof

_____ 6. Having a variety of characteristics, abilities, or appearances

_____ 7. Clothes

_____ 8. A closed four-wheeled carriage with an open driver's seat in front

_____ 9. Incapable of being corrected or reformed

_____ 10. Rejects the validity or authority of

_____ 11. A block or slab on which a pedestal, column or statue is placed

_____ 12. Courageously noble

_____ 13. Begging

_____ 14. Sleepwalker

_____ 15. Rashly or wastefully extravagant

_____ 16. Not allowing contradiction or refusal; commanding

_____ 17. A place or condition of suffering, expiation or remorse

_____ 18. Something that is airy, insubstantial or passing

_____ 19. Sloppy; slovenly

_____ 20. Impulsive and passionate

Pygmalion Vocabulary Fill In The Blanks 3 Answer Key

ASUNDER	1. Apart from each other in position or direction
AMIABLE	2. Friendly and agreeable
DOGMATICALLY	3. Characterized by an authoritative, arrogant assertion of unproved or unprovable principles
BILIOUS	4. Appearing as if experiencing gastric distress caused by a disorder of the liver
REMONSTRANCE	5. An expression of protest, complaint or reproof
MISCELLANEOUS	6. Having a variety of characteristics, abilities, or appearances
TOGS	7. Clothes
BROUGHAM	8. A closed four-wheeled carriage with an open driver's seat in front
INCORRIGIBLE	9. Incapable of being corrected or reformed
REPUDIATES	10. Rejects the validity or authority of
PLINTH	11. A block or slab on which a pedestal, column or statue is placed
MAGNANIMOUS	12. Courageously noble
MENDACITY	13. Begging
SOMNAMBULIST	14. Sleepwalker
PRODIGAL	15. Rashly or wastefully extravagant
PEREMPTORILY	16. Not allowing contradiction or refusal; commanding
PURGATORY	17. A place or condition of suffering, expiation or remorse
ZEPHYR	18. Something that is airy, insubstantial or passing
FROWZY	19. Sloppy; slovenly
IMPETUOUS	20. Impulsive and passionate

Pygmalion Vocabulary Fill In The Blanks 4

1. A block or slab on which a pedestal, column or statue is placed
2. Impulsive and passionate
3. Not allowing contradiction or refusal; commanding
4. Apart from each other in position or direction
5. Sloppy; slovenly
6. Friendly and agreeable
7. Having a variety of characteristics, abilities, or appearances
8. Rejects the validity or authority of
9. Incapable of being corrected or reformed
10. Boldness or enterprise; initiative or aggressiveness
11. A place or condition of suffering, expiation or remorse
12. Characterized by an authoritative, arrogant assertion of unproved or unprovable principles
13. Sleepwalker
14. A closed four-wheeled carriage with an open driver's seat in front
15. Belittling
16. An expression of protest, complaint or reproof
17. Appearing as if experiencing gastric distress caused by a disorder of the liver
18. Rashly or wastefully extravagant
19. To descend to the level of one considered inferior
20. Something that is airy, insubstantial or passing

Pygmalion Vocabulary Fill In The Blanks 4 Answer Key

PLINTH	1. A block or slab on which a pedestal, column or statue is placed
IMPETUOUS	2. Impulsive and passionate
PEREMPTORILY	3. Not allowing contradiction or refusal; commanding
ASUNDER	4. Apart from each other in position or direction
FROWZY	5. Sloppy; slovenly
AMIABLE	6. Friendly and agreeable
MISCELLANEOUS	7. Having a variety of characteristics, abilities, or appearances
REPUDIATES	8. Rejects the validity or authority of
INCORRIGIBLE	9. Incapable of being corrected or reformed
GUMPTION	10. Boldness or enterprise; initiative or aggressiveness
PURGATORY	11. A place or condition of suffering, expiation or remorse
DOGMATICALLY	12. Characterized by an authoritative, arrogant assertion of unproved or unprovable principles
SOMNAMBULIST	13. Sleepwalker
BROUGHAM	14. A closed four-wheeled carriage with an open driver's seat in front
DEPRECIATING	15. Belittling
REMONSTRANCE	16. An expression of protest, complaint or reproof
BILIOUS	17. Appearing as if experiencing gastric distress caused by a disorder of the liver
PRODIGAL	18. Rashly or wastefully extravagant
CONDESCENSION	19. To descend to the level of one considered inferior
ZEPHYR	20. Something that is airy, insubstantial or passing

Pygmalion Vocabulary Matching 1

___ 1. ZEPHYR	A. Not allowing contradiction or refusal; commanding
___ 2. DEMEAN	B. Friendly and agreeable
___ 3. MENDACITY	C. Impulsive and passionate
___ 4. AMIABLE	D. Sleepwalker
___ 5. INCORRIGIBLE	E. A block or slab on which a pedestal, column or statue is placed
___ 6. MAGNANIMOUS	F. Apart from each other in position or direction
___ 7. REMONSTRANCE	G. Begging
___ 8. REPUDIATES	H. Something that is airy, insubstantial or passing
___ 9. PEREMPTORILY	I. A place or condition of suffering, expiation or remorse
___10. GUMPTION	J. A closed four-wheeled carriage with an open driver's seat in front
___11. PLINTH	K. Rejects the validity or authority of
___12. PEDANTIC	L. By the book; following the rules exactly
___13. FROWZY	M. Incapable of being corrected or reformed
___14. DEPRECIATING	N. Characterized by an authoritative, arrogant assertion of unproved or unprovable principles
___15. PURGATORY	O. To humble oneself
___16. ASUNDER	P. Boldness or enterprise; initiative or aggressiveness
___17. IMPETUOUS	Q. To descend to the level of one considered inferior
___18. SOMNAMBULIST	R. Appearing as if experiencing gastric distress caused by a disorder of the liver
___19. TOGS	S. Having a variety of characteristics, abilities, or appearances
___20. BROUGHAM	T. An expression of protest, complaint or reproof
___21. BILIOUS	U. Rashly or wastefully extravagant
___22. CONDESCENSION	V. Belittling
___23. MISCELLANEOUS	W. Clothes
___24. DOGMATICALLY	X. Courageously noble
___25. PRODIGAL	Y. Sloppy; slovenly

Pygmalion Vocabulary Matching 1 Answer Key

H - 1.	ZEPHYR	A. Not allowing contradiction or refusal; commanding
O - 2.	DEMEAN	B. Friendly and agreeable
G - 3.	MENDACITY	C. Impulsive and passionate
B - 4.	AMIABLE	D. Sleepwalker
M - 5.	INCORRIGIBLE	E. A block or slab on which a pedestal, column or statue is placed
X - 6.	MAGNANIMOUS	F. Apart from each other in position or direction
T - 7.	REMONSTRANCE	G. Begging
K - 8.	REPUDIATES	H. Something that is airy, insubstantial or passing
A - 9.	PEREMPTORILY	I. A place or condition of suffering, expiation or remorse
P - 10.	GUMPTION	J. A closed four-wheeled carriage with an open driver's seat in front
E - 11.	PLINTH	K. Rejects the validity or authority of
L - 12.	PEDANTIC	L. By the book; following the rules exactly
Y - 13.	FROWZY	M. Incapable of being corrected or reformed
V - 14.	DEPRECIATING	N. Characterized by an authoritative, arrogant assertion of unproved or unprovable principles
I - 15.	PURGATORY	O. To humble oneself
F - 16.	ASUNDER	P. Boldness or enterprise; initiative or aggressiveness
C - 17.	IMPETUOUS	Q. To descend to the level of one considered inferior
D - 18.	SOMNAMBULIST	R. Appearing as if experiencing gastric distress caused by a disorder of the liver
W - 19.	TOGS	S. Having a variety of characteristics, abilities, or appearances
J - 20.	BROUGHAM	T. An expression of protest, complaint or reproof
R - 21.	BILIOUS	U. Rashly or wastefully extravagant
Q - 22.	CONDESCENSION	V. Belittling
S - 23.	MISCELLANEOUS	W. Clothes
N - 24.	DOGMATICALLY	X. Courageously noble
U - 25.	PRODIGAL	Y. Sloppy; slovenly

Pygmalion Vocabulary Matching 2

___ 1. CONDESCENSION A. Impulsive and passionate
___ 2. ASUNDER B. Belittling
___ 3. REPUDIATES C. Not allowing contradiction or refusal; commanding
___ 4. DEPRECIATING D. Clothes
___ 5. IMPETUOUS E. Having a variety of characteristics, abilities, or appearances
___ 6. PLINTH F. An expression of protest, complaint or reproof
___ 7. PEREMPTORILY G. A closed four-wheeled carriage with an open driver's seat in front
___ 8. PRODIGAL H. Sleepwalker
___ 9. DOGMATICALLY I. Rejects the validity or authority of
___10. TOGS J. By the book; following the rules exactly
___11. BROUGHAM K. Appearing as if experiencing gastric distress caused by a disorder of the liver
___12. ZEPHYR L. To descend to the level of one considered inferior
___13. PEDANTIC M. A block or slab on which a pedestal, column or statue is placed
___14. AMIABLE N. Sloppy; slovenly
___15. MAGNANIMOUS O. Courageously noble
___16. GUMPTION P. Friendly and agreeable
___17. INCORRIGIBLE Q. Boldness or enterprise; initiative or aggressiveness
___18. FROWZY R. To humble oneself
___19. MISCELLANEOUS S. Incapable of being corrected or reformed
___20. SOMNAMBULIST T. Something that is airy, insubstantial or passing
___21. DEMEAN U. Begging
___22. MENDACITY V. Apart from each other in position or direction
___23. REMONSTRANCE W. Characterized by an authoritative, arrogant assertion of unproved or unprovable principles
___24. BILIOUS X. A place or condition of suffering, expiation or remorse
___25. PURGATORY Y. Rashly or wastefully extravagant

Pygmalion Vocabulary Matching 2 Answer Key

L - 1.	CONDESCENSION	A. Impulsive and passionate
V - 2.	ASUNDER	B. Belittling
I - 3.	REPUDIATES	C. Not allowing contradiction or refusal; commanding
B - 4.	DEPRECIATING	D. Clothes
A - 5.	IMPETUOUS	E. Having a variety of characteristics, abilities, or appearances
M - 6.	PLINTH	F. An expression of protest, complaint or reproof
C - 7.	PEREMPTORILY	G. A closed four-wheeled carriage with an open driver's seat in front
Y - 8.	PRODIGAL	H. Sleepwalker
W - 9.	DOGMATICALLY	I. Rejects the validity or authority of
D - 10.	TOGS	J. By the book; following the rules exactly
G - 11.	BROUGHAM	K. Appearing as if experiencing gastric distress caused by a disorder of the liver
T - 12.	ZEPHYR	L. To descend to the level of one considered inferior
J - 13.	PEDANTIC	M. A block or slab on which a pedestal, column or statue is placed
P - 14.	AMIABLE	N. Sloppy; slovenly
O - 15.	MAGNANIMOUS	O. Courageously noble
Q - 16.	GUMPTION	P. Friendly and agreeable
S - 17.	INCORRIGIBLE	Q. Boldness or enterprise; initiative or aggressiveness
N - 18.	FROWZY	R. To humble oneself
E - 19.	MISCELLANEOUS	S. Incapable of being corrected or reformed
H - 20.	SOMNAMBULIST	T. Something that is airy, insubstantial or passing
R - 21.	DEMEAN	U. Begging
U - 22.	MENDACITY	V. Apart from each other in position or direction
F - 23.	REMONSTRANCE	W. Characterized by an authoritative, arrogant assertion of unproved or unprovable principles
K - 24.	BILIOUS	X. A place or condition of suffering, expiation or remorse
X - 25.	PURGATORY	Y. Rashly or wastefully extravagant

Pygmalion Vocabulary Matching 3

___ 1. PEDANTIC   A. By the book; following the rules exactly
___ 2. ASUNDER   B. Apart from each other in position or direction
___ 3. MAGNANIMOUS   C. An expression of protest, complaint or reproof
___ 4. FROWZY   D. Friendly and agreeable
___ 5. DEPRECIATING   E. To humble oneself
___ 6. DOGMATICALLY   F. Belittling
___ 7. TOGS   G. Incapable of being corrected or reformed
___ 8. GUMPTION   H. Courageously noble
___ 9. PURGATORY   I. To descend to the level of one considered inferior
___10. PRODIGAL   J. Appearing as if experiencing gastric distress caused by a disorder of the liver
___11. DEMEAN   K. Not allowing contradiction or refusal; commanding
___12. ZEPHYR   L. Clothes
___13. SOMNAMBULIST   M. Sloppy; slovenly
___14. MISCELLANEOUS   N. Impulsive and passionate
___15. CONDESCENSION   O. Sleepwalker
___16. PLINTH   P. Something that is airy, insubstantial or passing
___17. BILIOUS   Q. A place or condition of suffering, expiation or remorse
___18. REMONSTRANCE   R. Begging
___19. INCORRIGIBLE   S. Having a variety of characteristics, abilities, or appearances
___20. PEREMPTORILY   T. A block or slab on which a pedestal, column or statue is placed
___21. AMIABLE   U. Rashly or wastefully extravagant
___22. REPUDIATES   V. Rejects the validity or authority of
___23. MENDACITY   W. Boldness or enterprise; initiative or aggressiveness
___24. BROUGHAM   X. A closed four-wheeled carriage with an open driver's seat in front
___25. IMPETUOUS   Y. Characterized by an authoritative, arrogant assertion of unproved or unprovable principles

Pygmalion Vocabulary Matching 3 Answer Key

A - 1. PEDANTIC	A.	By the book; following the rules exactly
B - 2. ASUNDER	B.	Apart from each other in position or direction
H - 3. MAGNANIMOUS	C.	An expression of protest, complaint or reproof
M - 4. FROWZY	D.	Friendly and agreeable
F - 5. DEPRECIATING	E.	To humble oneself
Y - 6. DOGMATICALLY	F.	Belittling
L - 7. TOGS	G.	Incapable of being corrected or reformed
W - 8. GUMPTION	H.	Courageously noble
Q - 9. PURGATORY	I.	To descend to the level of one considered inferior
U - 10. PRODIGAL	J.	Appearing as if experiencing gastric distress caused by a disorder of the liver
E - 11. DEMEAN	K.	Not allowing contradiction or refusal; commanding
P - 12. ZEPHYR	L.	Clothes
O - 13. SOMNAMBULIST	M.	Sloppy; slovenly
S - 14. MISCELLANEOUS	N.	Impulsive and passionate
I - 15. CONDESCENSION	O.	Sleepwalker
T - 16. PLINTH	P.	Something that is airy, insubstantial or passing
J - 17. BILIOUS	Q.	A place or condition of suffering, expiation or remorse
C - 18. REMONSTRANCE	R.	Begging
G - 19. INCORRIGIBLE	S.	Having a variety of characteristics, abilities, or appearances
K - 20. PEREMPTORILY	T.	A block or slab on which a pedestal, column or statue is placed
D - 21. AMIABLE	U.	Rashly or wastefully extravagant
V - 22. REPUDIATES	V.	Rejects the validity or authority of
R - 23. MENDACITY	W.	Boldness or enterprise; initiative or aggressiveness
X - 24. BROUGHAM	X.	A closed four-wheeled carriage with an open driver's seat in front
N - 25. IMPETUOUS	Y.	Characterized by an authoritative, arrogant assertion of unproved or unprovable principles

Pygmalion Vocabulary Matching 4

___ 1. IMPETUOUS
___ 2. REMONSTRANCE
___ 3. CONDESCENSION
___ 4. MENDACITY
___ 5. REPUDIATES
___ 6. FROWZY
___ 7. TOGS
___ 8. ZEPHYR
___ 9. BILIOUS
___ 10. SOMNAMBULIST
___ 11. DEPRECIATING
___ 12. MAGNANIMOUS
___ 13. PRODIGAL
___ 14. ASUNDER
___ 15. INCORRIGIBLE
___ 16. PEDANTIC
___ 17. BROUGHAM
___ 18. GUMPTION
___ 19. DEMEAN
___ 20. PLINTH
___ 21. PEREMPTORILY
___ 22. AMIABLE
___ 23. MISCELLANEOUS
___ 24. PURGATORY
___ 25. DOGMATICALLY

A. Boldness or enterprise; initiative or aggressiveness
B. Characterized by an authoritative, arrogant assertion of unproved or unprovable principles
C. A place or condition of suffering, expiation or remorse
D. By the book; following the rules exactly
E. Clothes
F. Having a variety of characteristics, abilities, or appearances
G. Friendly and agreeable
H. Begging
I. Something that is airy, insubstantial or passing
J. Sleepwalker
K. Rashly or wastefully extravagant
L. Rejects the validity or authority of
M. Impulsive and passionate
N. Courageously noble
O. An expression of protest, complaint or reproof
P. Appearing as if experiencing gastric distress caused by a disorder of the liver
Q. To humble oneself
R. A closed four-wheeled carriage with an open driver's seat in front
S. Apart from each other in position or direction
T. To descend to the level of one considered inferior
U. Sloppy; slovenly
V. Not allowing contradiction or refusal; commanding
W. Belittling
X. Incapable of being corrected or reformed
Y. A block or slab on which a pedestal, column or statue is placed

Pygmalion Vocabulary Matching 4 Answer Key

M - 1.	IMPETUOUS	A.	Boldness or enterprise; initiative or aggressiveness
O - 2.	REMONSTRANCE	B.	Characterized by an authoritative, arrogant assertion of unproved or unprovable principles
T - 3.	CONDESCENSION	C.	A place or condition of suffering, expiation or remorse
H - 4.	MENDACITY	D.	By the book; following the rules exactly
L - 5.	REPUDIATES	E.	Clothes
U - 6.	FROWZY	F.	Having a variety of characteristics, abilities, or appearances
E - 7.	TOGS	G.	Friendly and agreeable
I - 8.	ZEPHYR	H.	Begging
P - 9.	BILIOUS	I.	Something that is airy, insubstantial or passing
J - 10.	SOMNAMBULIST	J.	Sleepwalker
W - 11.	DEPRECIATING	K.	Rashly or wastefully extravagant
N - 12.	MAGNANIMOUS	L.	Rejects the validity or authority of
K - 13.	PRODIGAL	M.	Impulsive and passionate
S - 14.	ASUNDER	N.	Courageously noble
X - 15.	INCORRIGIBLE	O.	An expression of protest, complaint or reproof
D - 16.	PEDANTIC	P.	Appearing as if experiencing gastric distress caused by a disorder of the liver
R - 17.	BROUGHAM	Q.	To humble oneself
A - 18.	GUMPTION	R.	A closed four-wheeled carriage with an open driver's seat in front
Q - 19.	DEMEAN	S.	Apart from each other in position or direction
Y - 20.	PLINTH	T.	To descend to the level of one considered inferior
V - 21.	PEREMPTORILY	U.	Sloppy; slovenly
G - 22.	AMIABLE	V.	Not allowing contradiction or refusal; commanding
F - 23.	MISCELLANEOUS	W.	Belittling
C - 24.	PURGATORY	X.	Incapable of being corrected or reformed
B - 25.	DOGMATICALLY	Y.	A block or slab on which a pedestal, column or statue is placed

Pygmalion Vocabulary Magic Squares 1

Match the definition with the vocabulary word. Put your answers in the magic squares below. When your answers are correct, all columns and rows will add to the same number.

A. DOGMATICALLY
B. DEMEAN
C. MISCELLANEOUS
D. CONDESCENSION
E. FROWZY
F. BILIOUS
G. PURGATORY
H. TOGS
I. ZEPHYR
J. BROUGHAM
K. PEDANTIC
L. REMONSTRANCE
M. DEPRECIATING
N. REPUDIATES
O. PRODIGAL
P. SOMNAMBULIST

1. Characterized by an authoritative, arrogant assertion of unproved or unprovable principles
2. Rejects the validity or authority of
3. A closed four-wheeled carriage with an open driver's seat in front
4. Sloppy; slovenly
5. A place or condition of suffering, expiation or remorse
6. An expression of protest, complaint or reproof
7. Sleepwalker
8. Having a variety of characteristics, abilities, or appearances
9. Rashly or wastefully extravagant
10. To descend to the level of one considered inferior
11. Clothes
12. By the book; following the rules exactly
13. Something that is airy, insubstantial or passing
14. Appearing as if experiencing gastric distress caused by a disorder of the liver
15. To humble oneself
16. Belittling

A=	B=	C=	D=
E=	F=	G=	H=
I=	J=	K=	L=
M=	N=	O=	P=

Pygmalion Vocabulary Magic Squares 1 Answer Key

Match the definition with the vocabulary word. Put your answers in the magic squares below. When your answers are correct, all columns and rows will add to the same number.

A. DOGMATICALLY
B. DEMEAN
C. MISCELLANEOUS
D. CONDESCENSION
E. FROWZY
F. BILIOUS
G. PURGATORY
H. TOGS
I. ZEPHYR
J. BROUGHAM
K. PEDANTIC
L. REMONSTRANCE
M. DEPRECIATING
N. REPUDIATES
O. PRODIGAL
P. SOMNAMBULIST

1. Characterized by an authoritative, arrogant assertion of unproved or unprovable principles
2. Rejects the validity or authority of
3. A closed four-wheeled carriage with an open driver's seat in front
4. Sloppy; slovenly
5. A place or condition of suffering, expiation or remorse
6. An expression of protest, complaint or reproof
7. Sleepwalker
8. Having a variety of characteristics, abilities, or appearances
9. Rashly or wastefully extravagant
10. To descend to the level of one considered inferior
11. Clothes
12. By the book; following the rules exactly
13. Something that is airy, insubstantial or passing
14. Appearing as if experiencing gastric distress caused by a disorder of the liver
15. To humble oneself
16. Belittling

A=1	B=15	C=8	D=10
E=4	F=14	G=5	H=11
I=13	J=3	K=12	L=6
M=16	N=2	O=9	P=7

Pygmalion Vocabulary Magic Squares 2

Match the definition with the vocabulary word. Put your answers in the magic squares below. When your answers are correct, all columns and rows will add to the same number.

A. PEREMPTORILY
B. REMONSTRANCE
C. DEMEAN
D. DOGMATICALLY
E. INCORRIGIBLE
F. PRODIGAL
G. BILIOUS
H. ASUNDER
I. MENDACITY
J. SOMNAMBULIST
K. FROWZY
L. GUMPTION
M. REPUDIATES
N. ZEPHYR
O. CONDESCENSION
P. PURGATORY

1. Apart from each other in position or direction
2. Rejects the validity or authority of
3. An expression of protest, complaint or reproof
4. Sloppy; slovenly
5. Sleepwalker
6. To humble oneself
7. A place or condition of suffering, expiation or remorse
8. Incapable of being corrected or reformed
9. To descend to the level of one considered inferior
10. Rashly or wastefully extravagant
11. Begging
12. Characterized by an authoritative, arrogant assertion of unproved or unprovable principles
13. Not allowing contradiction or refusal; commanding
14. Boldness or enterprise; initiative or aggressiveness
15. Appearing as if experiencing gastric distress caused by a disorder of the liver
16. Something that is airy, insubstantial or passing

A=	B=	C=	D=
E=	F=	G=	H=
I=	J=	K=	L=
M=	N=	O=	P=

Pygmalion Vocabulary Magic Squares 2 Answer Key

Match the definition with the vocabulary word. Put your answers in the magic squares below. When your answers are correct, all columns and rows will add to the same number.

A. PEREMPTORILY
B. REMONSTRANCE
C. DEMEAN
D. DOGMATICALLY
E. INCORRIGIBLE
F. PRODIGAL
G. BILIOUS
H. ASUNDER
I. MENDACITY
J. SOMNAMBULIST
K. FROWZY
L. GUMPTION
M. REPUDIATES
N. ZEPHYR
O. CONDESCENSION
P. PURGATORY

1. Apart from each other in position or direction
2. Rejects the validity or authority of
3. An expression of protest, complaint or reproof
4. Sloppy; slovenly
5. Sleepwalker
6. To humble oneself
7. A place or condition of suffering, expiation or remorse
8. Incapable of being corrected or reformed
9. To descend to the level of one considered inferior
10. Rashly or wastefully extravagant
11. Begging
12. Characterized by an authoritative, arrogant assertion of unproved or unprovable principles
13. Not allowing contradiction or refusal; commanding
14. Boldness or enterprise; initiative or aggressiveness
15. Appearing as if experiencing gastric distress caused by a disorder of the liver
16. Something that is airy, insubstantial or passing

A=13	B=3	C=6	D=12
E=8	F=10	G=15	H=1
I=11	J=5	K=4	L=14
M=2	N=16	O=9	P=7

Pygmalion Vocabulary Magic Squares 3

Match the definition with the vocabulary word. Put your answers in the magic squares below. When your answers are correct, all columns and rows will add to the same number.

A. PURGATORY
B. SOMNAMBULIST
C. CONDESCENSION
D. FROWZY
E. PEDANTIC
F. PEREMPTORILY
G. REMONSTRANCE
H. DEMEAN
I. DOGMATICALLY
J. BROUGHAM
K. IMPETUOUS
L. PLINTH
M. ZEPHYR
N. MISCELLANEOUS
O. DEPRECIATING
P. PRODIGAL

1. To descend to the level of one considered inferior
2. A closed four-wheeled carriage with an open driver's seat in front
3. Not allowing contradiction or refusal; commanding
4. Belittling
5. Rashly or wastefully extravagant
6. By the book; following the rules exactly
7. Characterized by an authoritative, arrogant assertion of unproved or unprovable principles
8. Sloppy; slovenly
9. Something that is airy, insubstantial or passing
10. To humble oneself
11. A block or slab on which a pedestal, column or statue is placed
12. A place or condition of suffering, expiation or remorse
13. Sleepwalker
14. Impulsive and passionate
15. An expression of protest, complaint or reproof
16. Having a variety of characteristics, abilities, or appearances

A=	B=	C=	D=
E=	F=	G=	H=
I=	J=	K=	L=
M=	N=	O=	P=

Pygmalion Vocabulary Magic Squares 3 Answer Key

Match the definition with the vocabulary word. Put your answers in the magic squares below. When your answers are correct, all columns and rows will add to the same number.

A. PURGATORY
B. SOMNAMBULIST
C. CONDESCENSION
D. FROWZY
E. PEDANTIC
F. PEREMPTORILY
G. REMONSTRANCE
H. DEMEAN
I. DOGMATICALLY
J. BROUGHAM
K. IMPETUOUS
L. PLINTH
M. ZEPHYR
N. MISCELLANEOUS
O. DEPRECIATING
P. PRODIGAL

1. To descend to the level of one considered inferior
2. A closed four-wheeled carriage with an open driver's seat in front
3. Not allowing contradiction or refusal; commanding
4. Belittling
5. Rashly or wastefully extravagant
6. By the book; following the rules exactly
7. Characterized by an authoritative, arrogant assertion of unproved or unprovable principles
8. Sloppy; slovenly
9. Something that is airy, insubstantial or passing
10. To humble oneself
11. A block or slab on which a pedestal, column or statue is placed
12. A place or condition of suffering, expiation or remorse
13. Sleepwalker
14. Impulsive and passionate
15. An expression of protest, complaint or reproof
16. Having a variety of characteristics, abilities, or appearances

A=12	B=13	C=1	D=8
E=6	F=3	G=15	H=10
I=7	J=2	K=14	L=11
M=9	N=16	O=4	P=5

Pygmalion Vocabulary Magic Squares 4

Match the definition with the vocabulary word. Put your answers in the magic squares below. When your answers are correct, all columns and rows will add to the same number.

A. AMIABLE
B. REPUDIATES
C. DEPRECIATING
D. CONDESCENSION
E. TOGS
F. SOMNAMBULIST
G. GUMPTION
H. DEMEAN
I. INCORRIGIBLE
J. IMPETUOUS
K. BROUGHAM
L. MISCELLANEOUS
M. REMONSTRANCE
N. PEREMPTORILY
O. PEDANTIC
P. MAGNANIMOUS

1. Rejects the validity or authority of
2. Boldness or enterprise; initiative or aggressiveness
3. A closed four-wheeled carriage with an open driver's seat in front
4. Not allowing contradiction or refusal; commanding
5. An expression of protest, complaint or reproof
6. Having a variety of characteristics, abilities, or appearances
7. To humble oneself
8. Friendly and agreeable
9. Courageously noble
10. Incapable of being corrected or reformed
11. Clothes
12. To descend to the level of one considered inferior
13. Belittling
14. Sleepwalker
15. Impulsive and passionate
16. By the book; following the rules exactly

A=	B=	C=	D=
E=	F=	G=	H=
I=	J=	K=	L=
M=	N=	O=	P=

Pygmalion Vocabulary Magic Squares 4 Answer Key

Match the definition with the vocabulary word. Put your answers in the magic squares below. When your answers are correct, all columns and rows will add to the same number.

A. AMIABLE
B. REPUDIATES
C. DEPRECIATING
D. CONDESCENSION
E. TOGS
F. SOMNAMBULIST
G. GUMPTION
H. DEMEAN
I. INCORRIGIBLE
J. IMPETUOUS
K. BROUGHAM
L. MISCELLANEOUS
M. REMONSTRANCE
N. PEREMPTORILY
O. PEDANTIC
P. MAGNANIMOUS

1. Rejects the validity or authority of
2. Boldness or enterprise; initiative or aggressiveness
3. A closed four-wheeled carriage with an open driver's seat in front
4. Not allowing contradiction or refusal; commanding
5. An expression of protest, complaint or reproof
6. Having a variety of characteristics, abilities, or appearances
7. To humble oneself
8. Friendly and agreeable
9. Courageously noble
10. Incapable of being corrected or reformed
11. Clothes
12. To descend to the level of one considered inferior
13. Belittling
14. Sleepwalker
15. Impulsive and passionate
16. By the book; following the rules exactly

A=8	B=1	C=13	D=12
E=11	F=14	G=2	H=7
I=10	J=15	K=3	L=6
M=5	N=4	O=16	P=9

Pygmalion Vocabulary Word Search 1

Words are placed backwards, forward, diagonally, up and down. Clues listed below can help you find the words. Circle the hidden vocabulary words in the maze.

```
M E L B I G I R R O C N I P N W G R N B
I A Q P I L Z P C T K S A E R T X E G K
S Q G H R L X W C O R O S R G W M M Y L
C I U N D O I G V G M M U E Y Z W O R F
E B M P A R D O B S V N N M Q R W N B H
L Z P P P N Q I U W Y A D P H N N S F Q
L V T M E M I S G S B M E T M K G T K P
A F I F E T W M N A M B R O D T G R C N
N V O L B N U R O K L U C R E K G A P N
E K N W R G D O K U C L R I P J L N L V
O B V R O N Y A U Q S I X L R M W C S M
U C T V U Q M R C S Z S R Y E B J E F W
S H J K G R Q W L I X T W X C Y Q Y V L
W D K M H K D H N Q T N N F I R X Y P K
F A T F A B S V D J S Y J Y A V Z C U Z
P M M Z M R X L N L S X F M T Z I B R C
T I M Z F D M S M Y C Z W K I T Z R G N
Z A C O N D E S C E N S I O N C E F A J
Y B G H G K W S C Y M R V A G F P Z T L
Y L L A C I T A M G O D D R S M H V O Z
R E P U D I A T E S F E R K K Y Y N R G
D E M E A N Y G X B P L I N T H R D Y L
```

A block or slab on which a pedestal, column or statue is placed (6)

A closed four-wheeled carriage with an open driver's seat in front (8)

A place or condition of suffering, expiation or remorse (9)

An expression of protest, complaint or reproof (12)

Apart from each other in position or direction (7)

Appearing as if experiencing gastric distress caused by a disorder of the liver (7)

Begging (9)

Belittling (12)

Boldness or enterprise; initiative or aggressiveness (8)

By the book; following the rules exactly (8)

Characterized by an authoritative, arrogant assertion of unproved or unprovable principles (12)

Clothes (4)

Courageously noble (11)

Friendly and agreeable (7)

Having a variety of characteristics, abilities, or appearances (13)

Impulsive and passionate (9)

Incapable of being corrected or reformed (12)

Not allowing contradiction or refusal; commanding (12)

Rashly or wastefully extravagant (8)

Rejects the validity or authority of (10)

Sleepwalker (12)

Sloppy; slovenly (6)

Something that is airy, insubstantial or passing (6)

To descend to the level of one considered inferior (13)

To humble oneself (6)

Pygmalion Vocabulary Word Search 1 Answer Key

Words are placed backwards, forward, diagonally, up and down. Clues listed below can help you find the words. Circle the hidden vocabulary words in the maze.

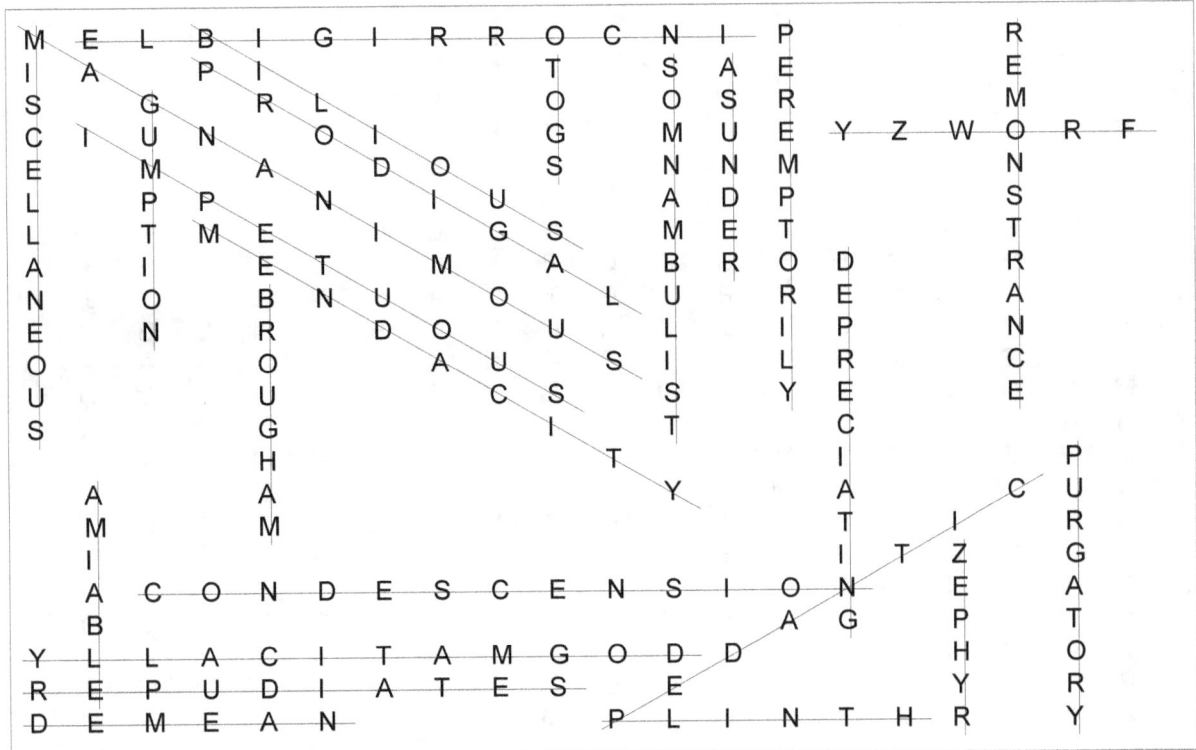

- A block or slab on which a pedestal, column or statue is placed (6)
- A closed four-wheeled carriage with an open driver's seat in front (8)
- A place or condition of suffering, expiation or remorse (9)
- An expression of protest, complaint or reproof (12)
- Apart from each other in position or direction (7)
- Appearing as if experiencing gastric distress caused by a disorder of the liver (7)
- Begging (9)
- Belittling (12)
- Boldness or enterprise; initiative or aggressiveness (8)
- By the book; following the rules exactly (8)
- Characterized by an authoritative, arrogant assertion of unproved or unprovable principles (12)
- Clothes (4)
- Courageously noble (11)
- Friendly and agreeable (7)
- Having a variety of characteristics, abilities, or appearances (13)
- Impulsive and passionate (9)
- Incapable of being corrected or reformed (12)
- Not allowing contradiction or refusal; commanding (12)
- Rashly or wastefully extravagant (8)
- Rejects the validity or authority of (10)
- Sleepwalker (12)
- Sloppy; slovenly (6)
- Something that is airy, insubstantial or passing (6)
- To descend to the level of one considered inferior (13)
- To humble oneself (6)

Pygmalion Vocabulary Word Search 2

Words are placed backwards, forward, diagonally, up and down. Clues listed below can help you find the words. Circle the hidden vocabulary words in the maze.

```
S P E D A N T I C V B W L R G C R M P M
O M T V M L G J Z N D A M N W O E A U Y
M E H N Q X B X N N G Z I K B N M G R H
N N Z L R E P U D I A T E S S D O N G R
A D F Q H S S J D C A R G U W E N A A D
M A F T W B S O T I I B S O L S S N T X
B C Y M Q M R N C B N H G E D C T I O M
U I X V W P H E S F C P X N Q E R M R J
L T Z F P K R Y P W O T Y A S N A O Y J
I Y D P P P J J J C R D C L P S N U B D
S F D G E J V F Z B R Q N L B I C S A P
T M O D X Y J Z B Q I G F E I O E T M D
K H G Y R J T K S T G C D C L N P D I K
J M M Z C T X V B W I K F S I K Q T A L
F R A W C B T M K Q B P Y I O G W R B H
F G T O Y D H W X K L R N M U M C R L D
Y L I R O T P M E R E P R M S G O T E P
D Q C F N C D J T D X Y P V Z U B M X X
Y S A I T H B P N P H T J M G P E N L D
B W L R N Q K U F P I F X H Y A K K Q F
L P L B X N S F E O G P A P N R X Q M Y
C Z Y V V A T Z N G I M P E T U O U S Q
```

A block or slab on which a pedestal, column or statue is placed (6)
A closed four-wheeled carriage with an open driver's seat in front (8)
A place or condition of suffering, expiation or remorse (9)
An expression of protest, complaint or reproof (12)
Apart from each other in position or direction (7)
Appearing as if experiencing gastric distress caused by a disorder of the liver (7)
Begging (9)
Belittling (12)
Boldness or enterprise; initiative or aggressiveness (8)
By the book; following the rules exactly (8)
Characterized by an authoritative, arrogant assertion of unproved or unprovable principles (12)
Clothes (4)

Courageously noble (11)
Friendly and agreeable (7)
Having a variety of characteristics, abilities, or appearances (13)
Impulsive and passionate (9)
Incapable of being corrected or reformed (12)
Not allowing contradiction or refusal; commanding (12)
Rashly or wastefully extravagant (8)
Rejects the validity or authority of (10)
Sleepwalker (12)
Sloppy; slovenly (6)
Something that is airy, insubstantial or passing (6)
To descend to the level of one considered inferior (13)
To humble oneself (6)

Pygmalion Vocabulary Word Search 2 Answer Key

Words are placed backwards, forward, diagonally, up and down. Clues listed below can help you find the words. Circle the hidden vocabulary words in the maze.

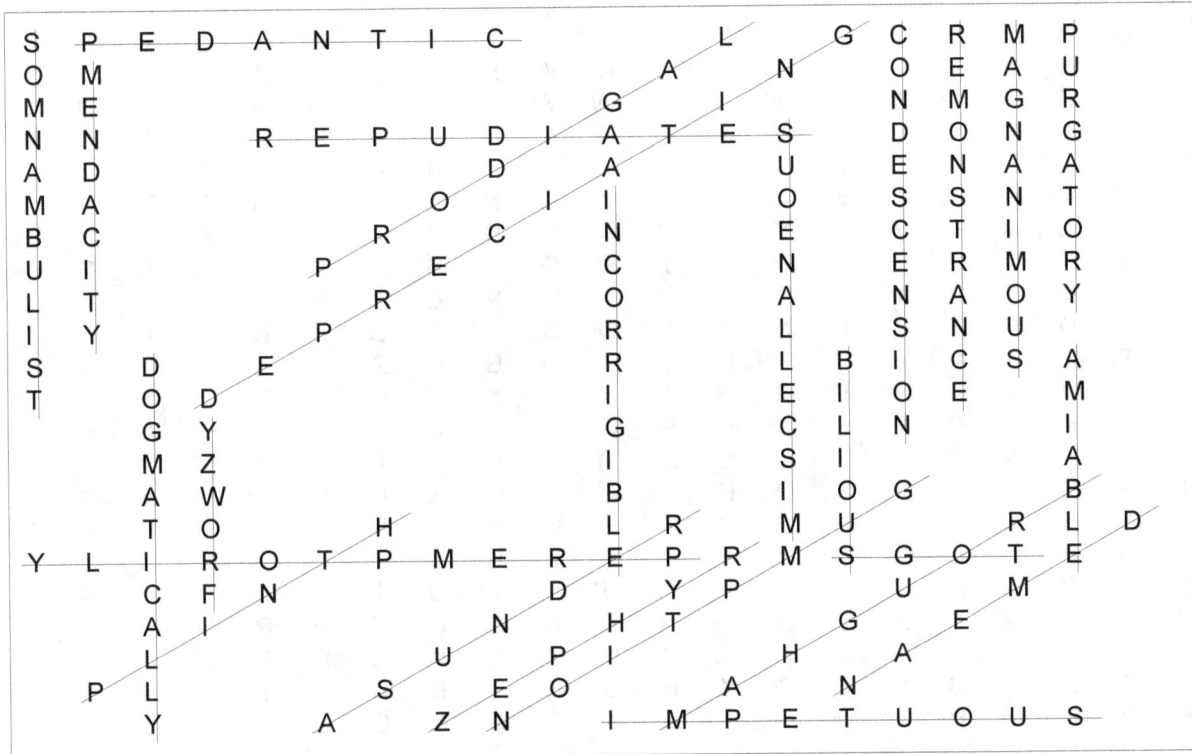

A block or slab on which a pedestal, column or statue is placed (6)
A closed four-wheeled carriage with an open driver's seat in front (8)
A place or condition of suffering, expiation or remorse (9)
An expression of protest, complaint or reproof (12)
Apart from each other in position or direction (7)
Appearing as if experiencing gastric distress caused by a disorder of the liver (7)
Begging (9)
Belittling (12)
Boldness or enterprise; initiative or aggressiveness (8)
By the book; following the rules exactly (8)
Characterized by an authoritative, arrogant assertion of unproved or unprovable principles (12)
Clothes (4)

Courageously noble (11)
Friendly and agreeable (7)
Having a variety of characteristics, abilities, or appearances (13)
Impulsive and passionate (9)
Incapable of being corrected or reformed (12)
Not allowing contradiction or refusal; commanding (12)
Rashly or wastefully extravagant (8)
Rejects the validity or authority of (10)
Sleepwalker (12)
Sloppy; slovenly (6)
Something that is airy, insubstantial or passing (6)
To descend to the level of one considered inferior (13)
To humble oneself (6)

Pygmalion Vocabulary Word Search 3

Words are placed backwards, forward, diagonally, up and down. Words listed below are included in the maze. Circle the hidden vocabulary words in the maze.

```
C O N D E S C E N S I O N X K W B D D F
V F G K G D F D X J N W F R K C Z F O T
D K Z P M Y W W G T W L Y T H K N G N
B R O U G H A M A G N A N I M O U S M T
P F J R I N C O R R I G I B L E Z D A Y
V N Q G M I S C E L L A N E O U S E T S
G B G A L Z Q Y K G H D S B Z S T P I Z
Z V V T B H Q T P J B D P B Y O B R C F
R S B O B V V C R R Y V P E X M T E A F
L C D R X Q F N K S O S R T D N D C L R
V T E Y D H P R E B Z D B L Z A B I L C
V M M Z X N B T G J R S I Z F M N A Y T
F H E Z C Y A U F R I G L G C B J T D M
Y M A N E I M B G J M O I F A U P I I V
J B N P D P E R E M P T O R I L Y N A C
S H B U T A H N B C E W U G I I Z G S Y
S N P I L M C Y J Z T X S N S W Y U C
L E O D M I J I R Z U T T Q J T O G N S
R N W N F A V D T G O H G L Y P R N D H
S M Q C X B Z P W Y U C C B G B F K E W
Z T Q F C L Z S Y H S D T D B L T S R C
F R P V R E M O N S T R A N C E J R S Z
```

AMIABLE	DOGMATICALLY	MISCELLANEOUS	REPUDIATES
ASUNDER	FROWZY	PEDANTIC	SOMNAMBULIST
BILIOUS	GUMPTION	PEREMPTORILY	TOGS
BROUGHAM	IMPETUOUS	PLINTH	ZEPHYR
CONDESCENSION	INCORRIGIBLE	PRODIGAL	
DEMEAN	MAGNANIMOUS	PURGATORY	
DEPRECIATING	MENDACITY	REMONSTRANCE	

Pygmalion Vocabulary Word Search 3 Answer Key

Words are placed backwards, forward, diagonally, up and down. Words listed below are included in the maze. Circle the hidden vocabulary words in the maze.

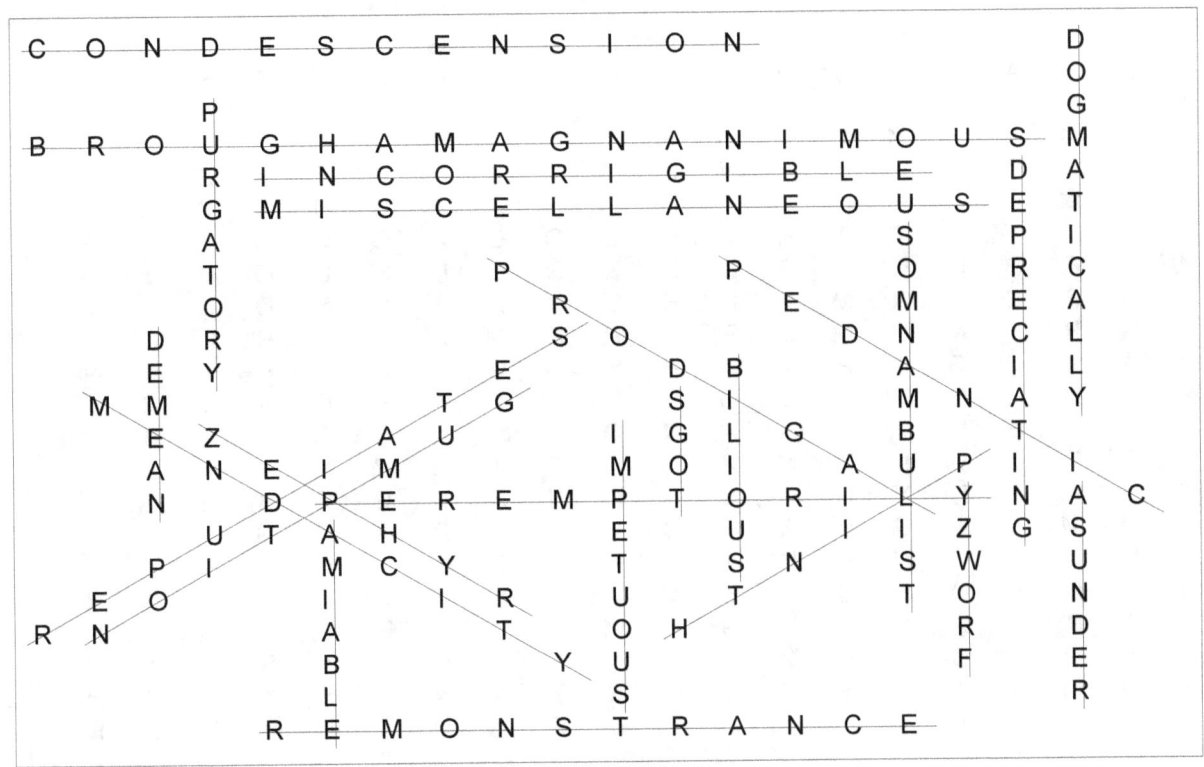

AMIABLE	DOGMATICALLY	MISCELLANEOUS	REPUDIATES
ASUNDER	FROWZY	PEDANTIC	SOMNAMBULIST
BILIOUS	GUMPTION	PEREMPTORILY	TOGS
BROUGHAM	IMPETUOUS	PLINTH	ZEPHYR
CONDESCENSION	INCORRIGIBLE	PRODIGAL	
DEMEAN	MAGNANIMOUS	PURGATORY	
DEPRECIATING	MENDACITY	REMONSTRANCE	

Pygmalion Vocabulary Word Search 4

Words are placed backwards, forward, diagonally, up and down. Words listed below are included in the maze. Circle the hidden vocabulary words in the maze.

```
D E P R E C I A T I N G H G G I D F H T
S E T A I D U P E R P V Y R J M E R R L
X M O Y V B Q Y F E M Q P N G P M O Z G
N Y G J P M Y P D E Z N M G Z E E W M T
M I S C E L L A N E O U S P M T A Z Y H
G H M Q G F N D P I W B B T R U N Y H P
W V H Y N T A H T D Z Q G H Q O Q H W B
W E F P I C Y P L H K S C M M U G H Y Q
F C F C I R M F K B L D K J L S D C K Y
H N R T N U M Z P E R E M P T O R I L Y
P A Y W G J P A H H F Q G L G N H W N N
X R H R C W X L G L S W T M P P M L R T
F T O E F W W A X N Q F A K U G J Q B M
B S P D W L Z M V M A T X N R X V B A J
V N F N I Y D I N K I N R N G Q B H W V
Z O M U G G B A H C L B I P A K G H G K
J M T S Y H A B A S P H Z M T U T K L V
H E B A Q H S L Z M C L S U O I L I B R
Z R P J Z R L E G J M V I R R U T Q D K
P T Q F C Y F W D G F X B N Y M S Q J G
S O M N A M B U L I S T M N T Y K P D H
I N C O R R I G I B L E W W K H P X D R
```

AMIABLE	DOGMATICALLY	MENDACITY	PURGATORY
ASUNDER	FROWZY	MISCELLANEOUS	REMONSTRANCE
BILIOUS	GUMPTION	PEDANTIC	REPUDIATES
BROUGHAM	IMPETUOUS	PEREMPTORILY	SOMNAMBULIST
DEMEAN	INCORRIGIBLE	PLINTH	TOGS
DEPRECIATING	MAGNANIMOUS	PRODIGAL	ZEPHYR

Pygmalion Vocabulary Word Search 4 Answer Key

Words are placed backwards, forward, diagonally, up and down. Words listed below are included in the maze. Circle the hidden vocabulary words in the maze.

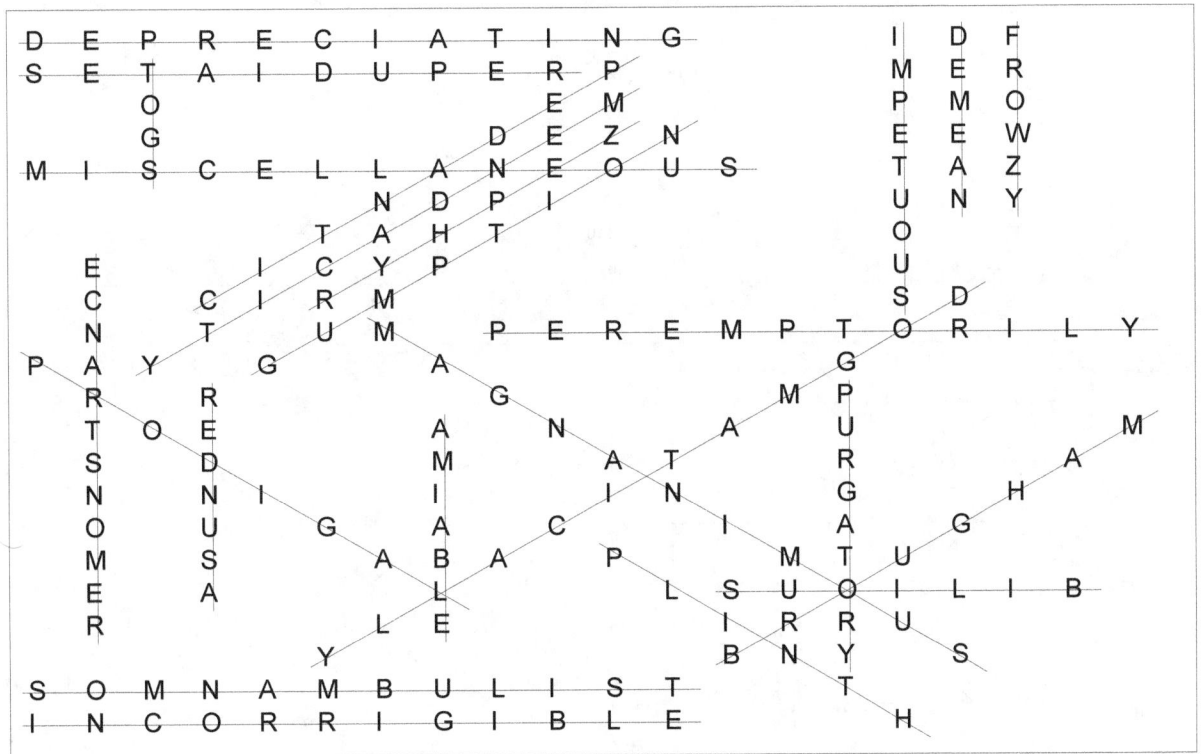

AMIABLE	DOGMATICALLY	MENDACITY	PURGATORY
ASUNDER	FROWZY	MISCELLANEOUS	REMONSTRANCE
BILIOUS	GUMPTION	PEDANTIC	REPUDIATES
BROUGHAM	IMPETUOUS	PEREMPTORILY	SOMNAMBULIST
DEMEAN	INCORRIGIBLE	PLINTH	TOGS
DEPRECIATING	MAGNANIMOUS	PRODIGAL	ZEPHYR

Pygmalion Vocabulary Crossword 1

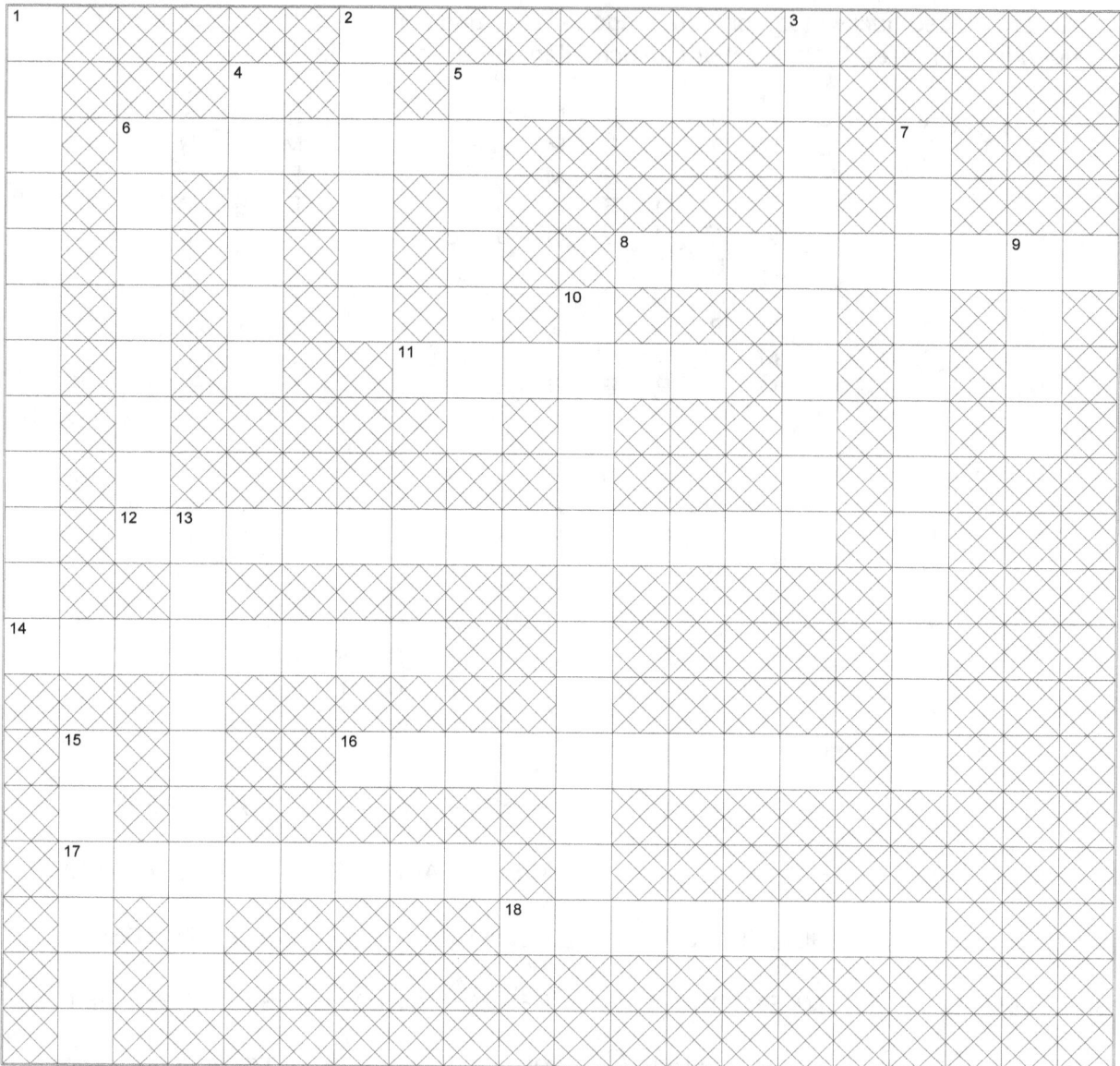

Across
5. Friendly and agreeable
6. Appearing as if experiencing gastric distress caused by a disorder of the liver
8. Begging
11. To humble oneself
12. Having a variety of characteristics, abilities, or appearances
14. Boldness or enterprise; initiative or aggressiveness
16. A place or condition of suffering, expiation or remorse
17. Rashly or wastefully extravagant
18. By the book; following the rules exactly

Down
1. Belittling
2. Sloppy; slovenly
3. Rejects the validity or authority of
4. A block or slab on which a pedestal, column or statue is placed
5. Apart from each other in position or direction
6. A closed four-wheeled carriage with an open driver's seat in front
7. Incapable of being corrected or reformed
9. Clothes
10. An expression of protest, complaint or reproof
13. Impulsive and passionate
15. Something that is airy, insubstantial or passing

Pygmalion Vocabulary Crossword 1 Answer Key

```
 1               2                       3
 D               F                       R
 E       4   P       R   5   A   M   I   A   B   L   E
 P   6   B   I   L   I   O   U   S               P   7   I
 R       R       I       W       U               U       N
 E       O       N       Z       N       8   M   E   N   D   A   C   I   T   9   Y
 C       U       T       Y       N      10   R       I       O       O
 I       G       T       Y      11   D   E   M   E   A   N       A       R       G
 A       H               H               R       M               T       R       S
 T       A                               M       O               E       I
 I      12  M  13  I   S   C   E   L   L   A   N   E   O   U   S       G
 N               M                               S                       I
14  G   U   M   P   T   I   O   N                 T                       B
                 E                               R                       L
            15   Z      16  P   U   R   G   A   T   O   R   Y           E
                 E      U
            17   P   R   O   D   I   G   A   L
                         18  P   E   D   A   N   T   I   C
                 H   U
                 Y   S
                     R
```

Across
5. Friendly and agreeable
6. Appearing as if experiencing gastric distress caused by a disorder of the liver
8. Begging
11. To humble oneself
12. Having a variety of characteristics, abilities, or appearances
14. Boldness or enterprise; initiative or aggressiveness
16. A place or condition of suffering, expiation or remorse
17. Rashly or wastefully extravagant
18. By the book; following the rules exactly

Down
1. Belittling
2. Sloppy; slovenly
3. Rejects the validity or authority of
4. A block or slab on which a pedestal, column or statue is placed
5. Apart from each other in position or direction
6. A closed four-wheeled carriage with an open driver's seat in front
7. Incapable of being corrected or reformed
9. Clothes
10. An expression of protest, complaint or reproof
13. Impulsive and passionate
15. Something that is airy, insubstantial or passing

Pygmalion Vocabulary Crossword 2

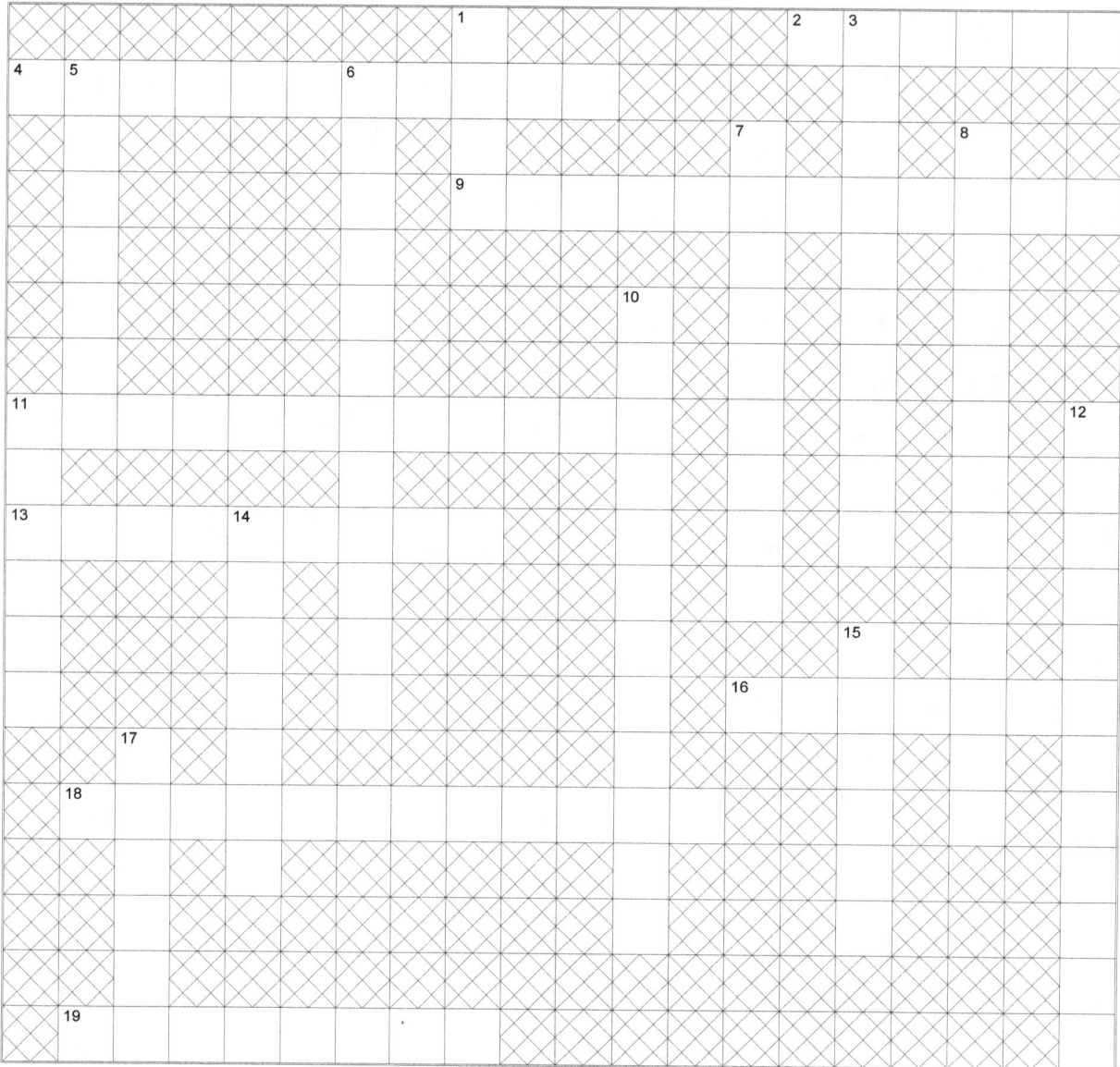

Across
2. Sloppy; slovenly
4. Courageously noble
9. Sleepwalker
11. Belittling
13. Begging
16. Appearing as if experiencing gastric distress caused by a disorder of the liver
18. Not allowing contradiction or refusal; commanding
19. Rashly or wastefully extravagant

Down
1. Clothes
3. Rejects the validity or authority of
5. Friendly and agreeable
6. Incapable of being corrected or reformed
7. Impulsive and passionate
8. Having a variety of characteristics, abilities, or appearances
10. Characterized by an authoritative, arrogant assertion of unproved or unprovable principles
11. To humble oneself
12. An expression of protest, complaint or reproof
14. Apart from each other in position or direction
15. A block or slab on which a pedestal, column or statue is placed
17. Something that is airy, insubstantial or passing

Pygmalion Vocabulary Crossword 2 Answer Key

							1 T				2 F	3 R	O	W	Z	Y
4 M	5 A	G	N	A	6 N	I	M	O	U	S		E				
	M				N		G			7 I		P		8 M		
	I				C		9 S	O	M	N	A	M	B	U	L	I	S	T
	A				O					P		D		I		S	
	B				R			10 D		E		I		C		
	L				R			O		T		A		E		
11 D	E	P	R	E	C	I	A	T	I	N	G		T		L		12 R
E					G			M		O			E		L		E
13 M	E	N	D	14 A	C	I	T	Y		M			A		S		A
E				S			B			A			U		S		A	N
A				U			L			T			S		15 P	E	
N				N			E			I		16 B	I	L	I	O	U	S
		17 Z		D						C			A			I		U	T
	18 P	E	R	E	M	P	T	O	R	I	L	Y			N		S	R
		P		R						L					T		A
		H								Y					H		N
		Y															C
	19 P	R	O	D	I	G	A	L									E

Across
2. Sloppy; slovenly
4. Courageously noble
9. Sleepwalker
11. Belittling
13. Begging
16. Appearing as if experiencing gastric distress caused by a disorder of the liver
18. Not allowing contradiction or refusal; commanding
19. Rashly or wastefully extravagant

Down
1. Clothes
3. Rejects the validity or authority of
5. Friendly and agreeable
6. Incapable of being corrected or reformed
7. Impulsive and passionate
8. Having a variety of characteristics, abilities, or appearances
10. Characterized by an authoritative, arrogant assertion of unproved or unprovable principles
11. To humble oneself
12. An expression of protest, complaint or reproof
14. Apart from each other in position or direction
15. A block or slab on which a pedestal, column or statue is placed
17. Something that is airy, insubstantial or passing

Pygmalion Vocabulary Crossword 3

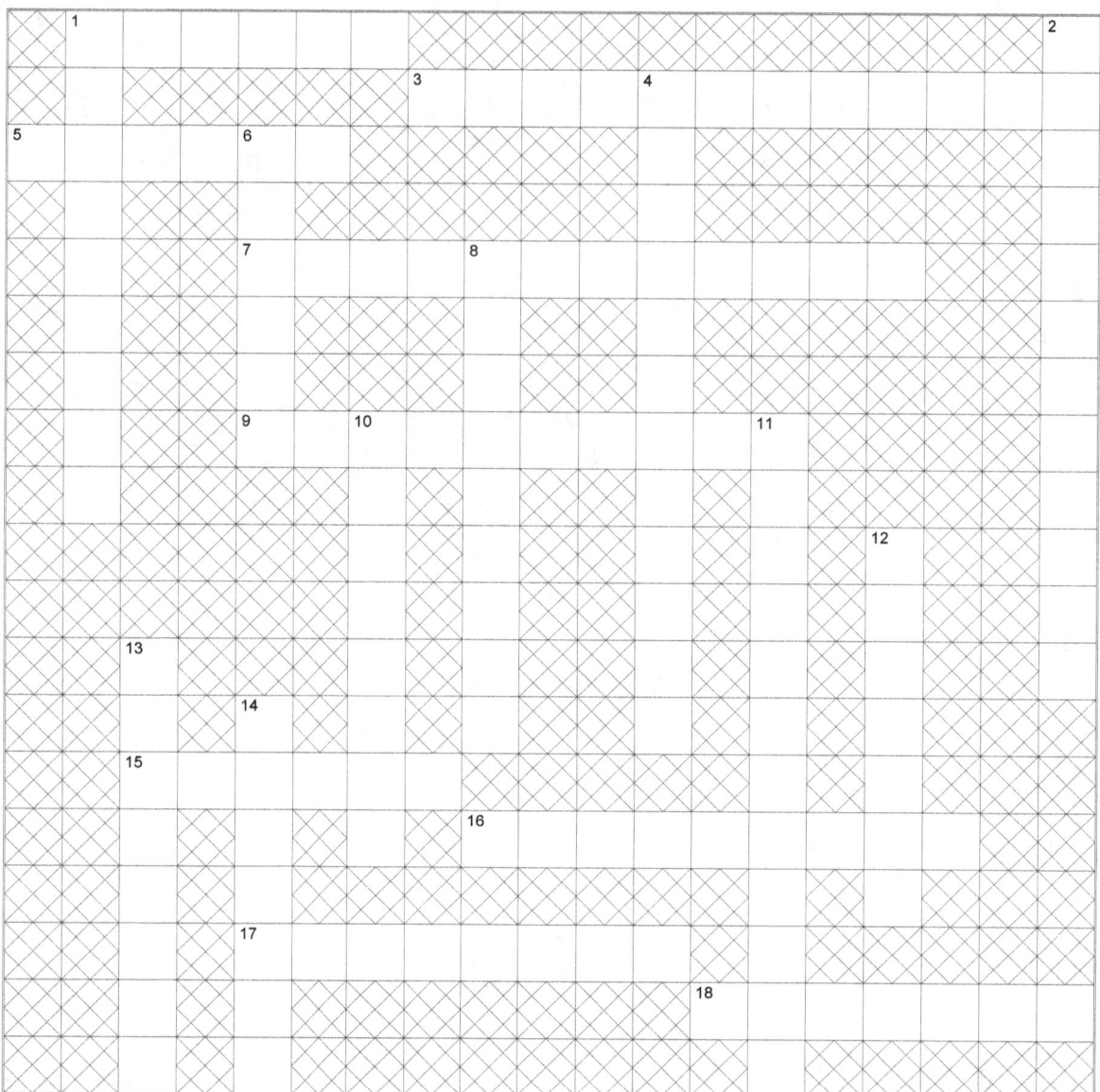

Across
1. A block or slab on which a pedestal, column or statue is placed
3. Incapable of being corrected or reformed
5. Sloppy; slovenly
7. Not allowing contradiction or refusal; commanding
9. Rejects the validity or authority of
15. To humble oneself
16. Impulsive and passionate
17. A closed four-wheeled carriage with an open driver's seat in front
18. Apart from each other in position or direction

Down
1. A place or condition of suffering, expiation or remorse
2. Belittling
4. An expression of protest, complaint or reproof
6. Something that is airy, insubstantial or passing
8. Begging
10. Rashly or wastefully extravagant
11. Sleepwalker
12. Appearing as if experiencing gastric distress caused by a disorder of the liver
13. By the book; following the rules exactly
14. Friendly and agreeable

Pygmalion Vocabulary Crossword 3 Answer Key

	1 P	L	I	N	T	H					4					2 D
	U						3 I	N	C	O	R	R	I	G	I	B	L	E
5 F	R	O	W	6 Z	Y						E					P
	G			E							M					R
	A			7 P	E	R	E	8 M	P	T	O	R	I	L	Y	E
	T			H				E			N					C
	O			Y				N			S					I
	R			9 R	E	10 P	U	D	I	A	T	E	11 S			A
	Y					R		A			R		O			T
						O		C			A		M	12 B		I
						D		I			N		N	I		N
		13 P				I		T			C		A	L		G
		E		14 A		G		Y			E		M	I		
		15 D	E	M	E	A	N						B	O		
		A		I		L		16 I	M	P	E	T	U	O	U	S
		N		A									L	S		
		T		17 B	R	O	U	G	H	A	M		I			
		I		L							18 A	S	U	N	D	E	R
		C		E							T					

Across
1. A block or slab on which a pedestal, column or statue is placed
3. Incapable of being corrected or reformed
5. Sloppy; slovenly
7. Not allowing contradiction or refusal; commanding
9. Rejects the validity or authority of
15. To humble oneself
16. Impulsive and passionate
17. A closed four-wheeled carriage with an open driver's seat in front
18. Apart from each other in position or direction

Down
1. A place or condition of suffering, expiation or remorse
2. Belittling
4. An expression of protest, complaint or reproof
6. Something that is airy, insubstantial or passing
8. Begging
10. Rashly or wastefully extravagant
11. Sleepwalker
12. Appearing as if experiencing gastric distress caused by a disorder of the liver
13. By the book; following the rules exactly
14. Friendly and agreeable

Pygmalion Vocabulary Crossword 4

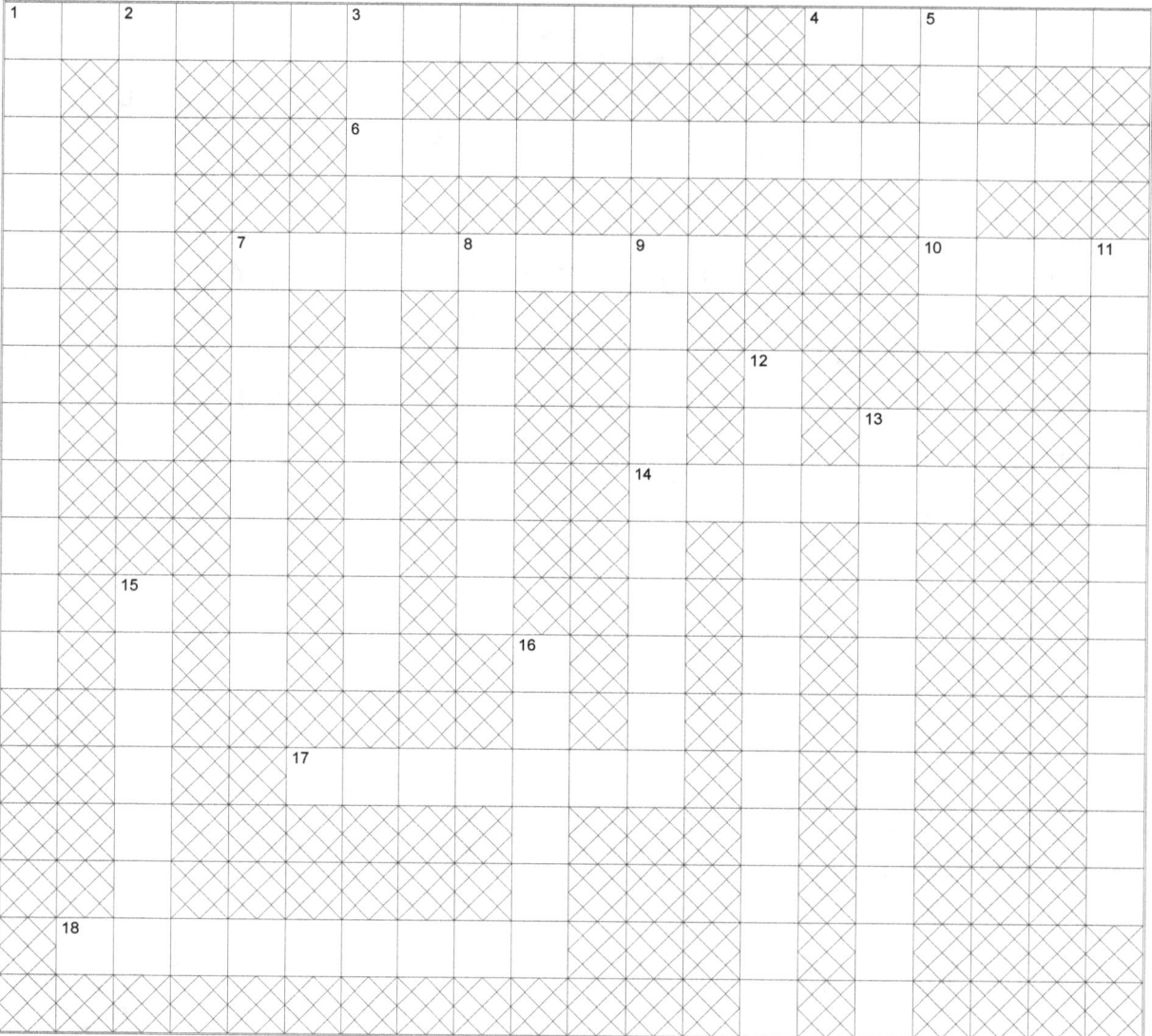

Across
1. Characterized by an authoritative, arrogant assertion of unproved or unprovable principles
4. Something that is airy, insubstantial or passing
6. To descend to the level of one considered inferior
7. A place or condition of suffering, expiation or remorse
10. Clothes
14. To humble oneself
17. Appearing as if experiencing gastric distress caused by a disorder of the liver
18. Begging

Down
1. Belittling
2. Boldness or enterprise; initiative or aggressiveness
3. Incapable of being corrected or reformed
5. A block or slab on which a pedestal, column or statue is placed
7. Rashly or wastefully extravagant
8. Apart from each other in position or direction
9. Rejects the validity or authority of
11. Sleepwalker
12. An expression of protest, complaint or reproof
13. Courageously noble
15. Friendly and agreeable
16. Sloppy; slovenly

Pygmalion Vocabulary Crossword 4 Answer Key

1 D	O	2 G	M	A	T	3 I	C	A	L	L	Y			4 Z	E	5 P	H	Y	R
E		U				N										L			
P		M				6 C	O	N	D	E	S	C	E	N	S	I	O	N	
R		P				O										N			
E		T		7 P	U	R	G	8 A	T	O	9 R	Y				10 T	O	G	11 S
C		I		R		R		S			E					H			O
I		O		O		I		U			P		12 R						M
A		N		D		G		N			U		E		13 M				N
T				I		I		D			14 D	E	M	E	A	N			A
I				G		B		E			I		O		G				M
N		15 A		A		L		R			A		N		N				B
G		M		L		E			16 F		T		S		A				U
		I							R		E		T		N				L
		A			17 B	I	L	I	O	U	S		R		I				I
		B							W				A		M				S
		L							Z				N		O				T
	18 M	E	N	D	A	C	I	T	Y				C		U				
													E		S				

Across
1. Characterized by an authoritative, arrogant assertion of unproved or unprovable principles
4. Something that is airy, insubstantial or passing
6. To descend to the level of one considered inferior
7. A place or condition of suffering, expiation or remorse
10. Clothes
14. To humble oneself
17. Appearing as if experiencing gastric distress caused by a disorder of the liver
18. Begging

.

Down
1. Belittling
2. Boldness or enterprise; initiative or aggressiveness
3. Incapable of being corrected or reformed
5. A block or slab on which a pedestal, column or statue is placed
7. Rashly or wastefully extravagant
8. Apart from each other in position or direction
9. Rejects the validity or authority of
11. Sleepwalker
12. An expression of protest, complaint or reproof
13. Courageously noble
15. Friendly and agreeable
16. Sloppy; slovenly

Pygmalion Vocabulary Juggle Letters 1

1. YACILTAMDOLG = 1. _____
Characterized by an authoritative, arrogant assertion of unproved or unprovable principles

2. HIPLTN = 2. _____
A block or slab on which a pedestal, column or statue is placed

3. ABMLIAE = 3. _____
Friendly and agreeable

4. SIMTUEOUP = 4. _____
Impulsive and passionate

5. TPDACNIE = 5. _____
By the book; following the rules exactly

6. EPRYZH = 6. _____
Something that is airy, insubstantial or passing

7. MEANED = 7. _____
To humble oneself

8. PNACEGIEIRDT = 8. _____
Belittling

9. ESOEIDSNNNOCC = 9. _____
To descend to the level of one considered inferior

10. ARUGOYRTP =10. _____
A place or condition of suffering, expiation or remorse

11. RNAUSDE =11. _____
Apart from each other in position or direction

12. MGUBHAOR =12. _____
A closed four-wheeled carriage with an open driver's seat in front

13. OWRYFZ =13. _____
Sloppy; slovenly

14. PMNUIOTG =14. _____
Boldness or enterprise; initiative or aggressiveness

15. SGOT =15. _____
Clothes

Pygmalion Vocabulary Juggle Letters 1 Answer Key

1. YACILTAMDOLG = 1. DOGMATICALLY
   Characterized by an authoritative, arrogant assertion of unproved or unprovable principles

2. HIPLTN = 2. PLINTH
   A block or slab on which a pedestal, column or statue is placed

3. ABMLIAE = 3. AMIABLE
   Friendly and agreeable

4. SIMTUEOUP = 4. IMPETUOUS
   Impulsive and passionate

5. TPDACNIE = 5. PEDANTIC
   By the book; following the rules exactly

6. EPRYZH = 6. ZEPHYR
   Something that is airy, insubstantial or passing

7. MEANED = 7. DEMEAN
   To humble oneself

8. PNACEGIEIRDT = 8. DEPRECIATING
   Belittling

9. ESOEIDSNNNOCC = 9. CONDESCENSION
   To descend to the level of one considered inferior

10. ARUGOYRTP = 10. PURGATORY
    A place or condition of suffering, expiation or remorse

11. RNAUSDE = 11. ASUNDER
    Apart from each other in position or direction

12. MGUBHAOR = 12. BROUGHAM
    A closed four-wheeled carriage with an open driver's seat in front

13. OWRYFZ = 13. FROWZY
    Sloppy; slovenly

14. PMNUIOTG = 14. GUMPTION
    Boldness or enterprise; initiative or aggressiveness

15. SGOT = 15. TOGS
    Clothes

Pygmalion Vocabulary Juggle Letters 2

1. GPATORYRU = 1. _____
A place or condition of suffering, expiation or remorse

2. LABEIAM = 2. _____
Friendly and agreeable

3. TIDECMAYN = 3. _____
Begging

4. LPHNIT = 4. _____
A block or slab on which a pedestal, column or statue is placed

5. NNCNOSECIOESD = 5. _____
To descend to the level of one considered inferior

6. LIOSIUB = 6. _____
Appearing as if experiencing gastric distress caused by a disorder of the liver

7. UIEPASTRED = 7. _____
Rejects the validity or authority of

8. OTLMCAYIALDG = 8. _____
Characterized by an authoritative, arrogant assertion of unproved or unprovable principles

9. OZYFRW = 9. _____
Sloppy; slovenly

10. SNUARED =10. _____
Apart from each other in position or direction

11. TDENPAIC =11. _____
By the book; following the rules exactly

12. TMUNGOPI =12. _____
Boldness or enterprise; initiative or aggressiveness

13. OANGNSIMMAU =13. _____
Courageously noble

14. NRRGILOBIECI =14. _____
Incapable of being corrected or reformed

15. SMOCELUSNLEAI =15. _____
Having a variety of characteristics, abilities, or appearances

Pygmalion Vocabulary Juggle Letters 2 Answer Key

1. GPATORYRU = 1. PURGATORY
A place or condition of suffering, expiation or remorse

2. LABEIAM = 2. AMIABLE
Friendly and agreeable

3. TIDECMAYN = 3. MENDACITY
Begging

4. LPHNIT = 4. PLINTH
A block or slab on which a pedestal, column or statue is placed

5. NNCNOSECIOESD = 5. CONDESCENSION
To descend to the level of one considered inferior

6. LIOSIUB = 6. BILIOUS
Appearing as if experiencing gastric distress caused by a disorder of the liver

7. UIEPASTRED = 7. REPUDIATES
Rejects the validity or authority of

8. OTLMCAYIALDG = 8. DOGMATICALLY
Characterized by an authoritative, arrogant assertion of unproved or unprovable principles

9. OZYFRW = 9. FROWZY
Sloppy; slovenly

10. SNUARED = 10. ASUNDER
Apart from each other in position or direction

11. TDENPAIC = 11. PEDANTIC
By the book; following the rules exactly

12. TMUNGOPI = 12. GUMPTION
Boldness or enterprise; initiative or aggressiveness

13. OANGNSIMMAU = 13. MAGNANIMOUS
Courageously noble

14. NRRGILOBIECI = 14. INCORRIGIBLE
Incapable of being corrected or reformed

15. SMOCELUSNLEAI = 15. MISCELLANEOUS
Having a variety of characteristics, abilities, or appearances

Pygmalion Vocabulary Juggle Letters 3

1. PTHLNI = 1. _____
A block or slab on which a pedestal, column or statue is placed

2. HERZPY = 2. _____
Something that is airy, insubstantial or passing

3. GSOT = 3. _____
Clothes

4. PETEIRUSDA = 4. _____
Rejects the validity or authority of

5. TPYEELMPRIRO = 5. _____
Not allowing contradiction or refusal; commanding

6. OZRFYW = 6. _____
Sloppy; slovenly

7. OREETRCMSANN = 7. _____
An expression of protest, complaint or reproof

8. IILOBUS = 8. _____
Appearing as if experiencing gastric distress caused by a disorder of the liver

9. RUASEND = 9. _____
Apart from each other in position or direction

10. MGLTLADYACIO = 10. _____
Characterized by an authoritative, arrogant assertion of unproved or unprovable principles

11. SECSINEONDNCO = 11. _____
To descend to the level of one considered inferior

12. LDORPGAI = 12. _____
Rashly or wastefully extravagant

13. IGNTOUPM = 13. _____
Boldness or enterprise; initiative or aggressiveness

14. BAIMEAL = 14. _____
Friendly and agreeable

15. MDEAEN = 15. _____
To humble oneself

Pygmalion Vocabulary Juggle Letters 3 Answer Key

1. PTHLNI = 1. PLINTH
A block or slab on which a pedestal, column or statue is placed

2. HERZPY = 2. ZEPHYR
Something that is airy, insubstantial or passing

3. GSOT = 3. TOGS
Clothes

4. PETEIRUSDA = 4. REPUDIATES
Rejects the validity or authority of

5. TPYEELMPRIRO = 5. PEREMPTORILY
Not allowing contradiction or refusal; commanding

6. OZRFYW = 6. FROWZY
Sloppy; slovenly

7. OREETRCMSANN = 7. REMONSTRANCE
An expression of protest, complaint or reproof

8. IILOBUS = 8. BILIOUS
Appearing as if experiencing gastric distress caused by a disorder of the liver

9. RUASEND = 9. ASUNDER
Apart from each other in position or direction

10. MGLTLADYACIO = 10. DOGMATICALLY
Characterized by an authoritative, arrogant assertion of unproved or unprovable principles

11. SECSINEONDNCO = 11. CONDESCENSION
To descend to the level of one considered inferior

12. LDORPGAI = 12. PRODIGAL
Rashly or wastefully extravagant

13. IGNTOUPM = 13. GUMPTION
Boldness or enterprise; initiative or aggressiveness

14. BAIMEAL = 14. AMIABLE
Friendly and agreeable

15. MDEAEN = 15. DEMEAN
To humble oneself

Pygmalion Vocabulary Juggle Letters 4

1. RCBIELRIOGNI = 1. _____
   Incapable of being corrected or reformed

2. RIOPPEYTLERM = 2. _____
   Not allowing contradiction or refusal; commanding

3. EPNCDAIT = 3. _____
   By the book; following the rules exactly

4. UPRIDEASET = 4. _____
   Rejects the validity or authority of

5. HAGMBUOR = 5. _____
   A closed four-wheeled carriage with an open driver's seat in front

6. SETOAMCNRENR = 6. _____
   An expression of protest, complaint or reproof

7. OGYCMALIDTLA = 7. _____
   Characterized by an authoritative, arrogant assertion of unproved or unprovable principles

8. RADPLIGO = 8. _____
   Rashly or wastefully extravagant

9. HEYPZR = 9. _____
   Something that is airy, insubstantial or passing

10. OTUGMPNI = 10. _____
    Boldness or enterprise; initiative or aggressiveness

11. CEITMAYDN = 11. _____
    Begging

12. EITGERDNPICA = 12. _____
    Belittling

13. UPTROGYAR = 13. _____
    A place or condition of suffering, expiation or remorse

14. EPTUMUSOI = 14. _____
    Impulsive and passionate

15. TSGO = 15. _____
    Clothes

Pygmalion Vocabulary Juggle Letters 4 Answer Key

1. RCBIELRIOGNI = 1. INCORRIGIBLE
   Incapable of being corrected or reformed

2. RIOPPEYTLERM = 2. PEREMPTORILY
   Not allowing contradiction or refusal; commanding

3. EPNCDAIT = 3. PEDANTIC
   By the book; following the rules exactly

4. UPRIDEASET = 4. REPUDIATES
   Rejects the validity or authority of

5. HAGMBUOR = 5. BROUGHAM
   A closed four-wheeled carriage with an open driver's seat in front

6. SETOAMCNRENR = 6. REMONSTRANCE
   An expression of protest, complaint or reproof

7. OGYCMALIDTLA = 7. DOGMATICALLY
   Characterized by an authoritative, arrogant assertion of unproved or unprovable principles

8. RADPLIGO = 8. PRODIGAL
   Rashly or wastefully extravagant

9. HEYPZR = 9. ZEPHYR
   Something that is airy, insubstantial or passing

10. OTUGMPNI = 10. GUMPTION
    Boldness or enterprise; initiative or aggressiveness

11. CEITMAYDN = 11. MENDACITY
    Begging

12. EITGERDNPICA = 12. DEPRECIATING
    Belittling

13. UPTROGYAR = 13. PURGATORY
    A place or condition of suffering, expiation or remorse

14. EPTUMUSOI = 14. IMPETUOUS
    Impulsive and passionate

15. TSGO = 15. TOGS
    Clothes

AMIABLE	Friendly and agreeable
ASUNDER	Apart from each other in position or direction
BILIOUS	Appearing as if experiencing gastric distress caused by a disorder of the liver
BROUGHAM	A closed four-wheeled carriage with an open driver's seat in front
CONDESCENSION	To descend to the level of one considered inferior
DEMEAN	To humble oneself

DEPRECIATING	Belittling
DOGMATICALLY	Characterized by an authoritative, arrogant assertion of unproved principles
FROWZY	Sloppy; slovenly
GUMPTION	Boldness or enterprise; initiative or aggressiveness
IMPETUOUS	Impulsive and passionate
INCORRIGIBLE	Incapable of being corrected or reformed

MAGNANIMOUS	Courageously noble
MENDACITY	Begging
MISCELLANEOUS	Having a variety of characteristics, abilities, or appearances
PEDANTIC	By the book; following the rules exactly
PEREMPTORILY	Not allowing contradiction or refusal; commanding
PLINTH	A block or slab on which a pedestal, column or statue is placed

PRODIGAL	Rashly or wastefully extravagant
PURGATORY	A place or condition of suffering, expiation or remorse
REMONSTRANCE	An expression of protest, complaint or reproof
REPUDIATES	Rejects the validity or authority of
SOMNAMBULIST	Sleepwalker
TOGS	Clothes

ZEPHYR	Something that is airy, insubstantial or passing

Pygmalion Vocabulary

GUMPTION	MENDACITY	BILIOUS	REMONSTRANCE	PEREMPTORILY
REPUDIATES	MAGNANIMOUS	SOMNAMBULIST	FROWZY	TOGS
DOGMATICALLY	BROUGHAM	FREE SPACE	MISCELLANEOUS	AMIABLE
PRODIGAL	INCORRIGIBLE	ASUNDER	PEDANTIC	DEPRECIATING
IMPETUOUS	ZEPHYR	DEMEAN	PLINTH	CONDESCENSION

Pygmalion Vocabulary

CONDESCENSION	PLINTH	DEMEAN	ZEPHYR	IMPETUOUS
DEPRECIATING	PEDANTIC	ASUNDER	INCORRIGIBLE	PRODIGAL
AMIABLE	MISCELLANEOUS	FREE SPACE	BROUGHAM	DOGMATICALLY
TOGS	FROWZY	SOMNAMBULIST	MAGNANIMOUS	REPUDIATES
PEREMPTORILY	REMONSTRANCE	BILIOUS	MENDACITY	GUMPTION

Pygmalion Vocabulary

PRODIGAL	REMONSTRANCE	DOGMATICALLY	ASUNDER	AMIABLE
BILIOUS	ZEPHYR	CONDESCENSION	TOGS	INCORRIGIBLE
REPUDIATES	DEMEAN	FREE SPACE	PURGATORY	MISCELLANEOUS
MENDACITY	DEPRECIATING	MAGNANIMOUS	PEREMPTORILY	PLINTH
BROUGHAM	SOMNAMBULIST	PEDANTIC	FROWZY	GUMPTION

Pygmalion Vocabulary

GUMPTION	FROWZY	PEDANTIC	SOMNAMBULIST	BROUGHAM
PLINTH	PEREMPTORILY	MAGNANIMOUS	DEPRECIATING	MENDACITY
MISCELLANEOUS	PURGATORY	FREE SPACE	DEMEAN	REPUDIATES
INCORRIGIBLE	TOGS	CONDESCENSION	ZEPHYR	BILIOUS
AMIABLE	ASUNDER	DOGMATICALLY	REMONSTRANCE	PRODIGAL

Pygmalion Vocabulary

DOGMATICALLY	DEPRECIATING	PLINTH	GUMPTION	DEMEAN
TOGS	PEREMPTORILY	AMIABLE	SOMNAMBULIST	REPUDIATES
BROUGHAM	MAGNANIMOUS	FREE SPACE	CONDESCENSION	PEDANTIC
MENDACITY	PRODIGAL	INCORRIGIBLE	PURGATORY	FROWZY
BILIOUS	REMONSTRANCE	MISCELLANEOUS	IMPETUOUS	ZEPHYR

Pygmalion Vocabulary

ZEPHYR	IMPETUOUS	MISCELLANEOUS	REMONSTRANCE	BILIOUS
FROWZY	PURGATORY	INCORRIGIBLE	PRODIGAL	MENDACITY
PEDANTIC	CONDESCENSION	FREE SPACE	MAGNANIMOUS	BROUGHAM
REPUDIATES	SOMNAMBULIST	AMIABLE	PEREMPTORILY	TOGS
DEMEAN	GUMPTION	PLINTH	DEPRECIATING	DOGMATICALLY

Pygmalion Vocabulary

PLINTH	BROUGHAM	GUMPTION	ASUNDER	TOGS
PURGATORY	CONDESCENSION	DEMEAN	PEDANTIC	MISCELLANEOUS
PRODIGAL	SOMNAMBULIST	FREE SPACE	DEPRECIATING	FROWZY
REPUDIATES	ZEPHYR	MENDACITY	REMONSTRANCE	BILIOUS
IMPETUOUS	AMIABLE	PEREMPTORILY	DOGMATICALLY	INCORRIGIBLE

Pygmalion Vocabulary

INCORRIGIBLE	DOGMATICALLY	PEREMPTORILY	AMIABLE	IMPETUOUS
BILIOUS	REMONSTRANCE	MENDACITY	ZEPHYR	REPUDIATES
FROWZY	DEPRECIATING	FREE SPACE	SOMNAMBULIST	PRODIGAL
MISCELLANEOUS	PEDANTIC	DEMEAN	CONDESCENSION	PURGATORY
TOGS	ASUNDER	GUMPTION	BROUGHAM	PLINTH

Pygmalion Vocabulary

CONDESCENSION	DEPRECIATING	DOGMATICALLY	GUMPTION	TOGS
PEREMPTORILY	ASUNDER	PLINTH	MENDACITY	PRODIGAL
MAGNANIMOUS	MISCELLANEOUS	FREE SPACE	BROUGHAM	REPUDIATES
AMIABLE	PEDANTIC	FROWZY	INCORRIGIBLE	REMONSTRANCE
DEMEAN	IMPETUOUS	ZEPHYR	PURGATORY	SOMNAMBULIST

Pygmalion Vocabulary

SOMNAMBULIST	PURGATORY	ZEPHYR	IMPETUOUS	DEMEAN
REMONSTRANCE	INCORRIGIBLE	FROWZY	PEDANTIC	AMIABLE
REPUDIATES	BROUGHAM	FREE SPACE	MISCELLANEOUS	MAGNANIMOUS
PRODIGAL	MENDACITY	PLINTH	ASUNDER	PEREMPTORILY
TOGS	GUMPTION	DOGMATICALLY	DEPRECIATING	CONDESCENSION

Pygmalion Vocabulary

ZEPHYR	DEPRECIATING	IMPETUOUS	DEMEAN	GUMPTION
PEDANTIC	PRODIGAL	REMONSTRANCE	MISCELLANEOUS	CONDESCENSION
SOMNAMBULIST	INCORRIGIBLE	FREE SPACE	PEREMPTORILY	FROWZY
AMIABLE	PLINTH	ASUNDER	PURGATORY	DOGMATICALLY
BROUGHAM	BILIOUS	REPUDIATES	MAGNANIMOUS	MENDACITY

Pygmalion Vocabulary

MENDACITY	MAGNANIMOUS	REPUDIATES	BILIOUS	BROUGHAM
DOGMATICALLY	PURGATORY	ASUNDER	PLINTH	AMIABLE
FROWZY	PEREMPTORILY	FREE SPACE	INCORRIGIBLE	SOMNAMBULIST
CONDESCENSION	MISCELLANEOUS	REMONSTRANCE	PRODIGAL	PEDANTIC
GUMPTION	DEMEAN	IMPETUOUS	DEPRECIATING	ZEPHYR

Pygmalion Vocabulary

PEDANTIC	AMIABLE	PURGATORY	BILIOUS	MENDACITY
PRODIGAL	PEREMPTORILY	REPUDIATES	TOGS	BROUGHAM
DEPRECIATING	DEMEAN	FREE SPACE	IMPETUOUS	SOMNAMBULIST
PLINTH	ZEPHYR	ASUNDER	MISCELLANEOUS	GUMPTION
MAGNANIMOUS	FROWZY	REMONSTRANCE	DOGMATICALLY	INCORRIGIBLE

Pygmalion Vocabulary

INCORRIGIBLE	DOGMATICALLY	REMONSTRANCE	FROWZY	MAGNANIMOUS
GUMPTION	MISCELLANEOUS	ASUNDER	ZEPHYR	PLINTH
SOMNAMBULIST	IMPETUOUS	FREE SPACE	DEMEAN	DEPRECIATING
BROUGHAM	TOGS	REPUDIATES	PEREMPTORILY	PRODIGAL
MENDACITY	BILIOUS	PURGATORY	AMIABLE	PEDANTIC

Pygmalion Vocabulary

PURGATORY	INCORRIGIBLE	ASUNDER	TOGS	BROUGHAM
PEDANTIC	REPUDIATES	FROWZY	GUMPTION	PRODIGAL
MISCELLANEOUS	MENDACITY	FREE SPACE	REMONSTRANCE	MAGNANIMOUS
ZEPHYR	CONDESCENSION	DOGMATICALLY	SOMNAMBULIST	IMPETUOUS
PEREMPTORILY	BILIOUS	AMIABLE	DEPRECIATING	DEMEAN

Pygmalion Vocabulary

DEMEAN	DEPRECIATING	AMIABLE	BILIOUS	PEREMPTORILY
IMPETUOUS	SOMNAMBULIST	DOGMATICALLY	CONDESCENSION	ZEPHYR
MAGNANIMOUS	REMONSTRANCE	FREE SPACE	MENDACITY	MISCELLANEOUS
PRODIGAL	GUMPTION	FROWZY	REPUDIATES	PEDANTIC
BROUGHAM	TOGS	ASUNDER	INCORRIGIBLE	PURGATORY

Pygmalion Vocabulary

GUMPTION	MISCELLANEOUS	CONDESCENSION	PRODIGAL	SOMNAMBULIST
PLINTH	BILIOUS	PEDANTIC	REMONSTRANCE	MENDACITY
ZEPHYR	DEMEAN	FREE SPACE	REPUDIATES	AMIABLE
TOGS	ASUNDER	MAGNANIMOUS	DOGMATICALLY	FROWZY
BROUGHAM	PURGATORY	DEPRECIATING	IMPETUOUS	PEREMPTORILY

Pygmalion Vocabulary

PEREMPTORILY	IMPETUOUS	DEPRECIATING	PURGATORY	BROUGHAM
FROWZY	DOGMATICALLY	MAGNANIMOUS	ASUNDER	TOGS
AMIABLE	REPUDIATES	FREE SPACE	DEMEAN	ZEPHYR
MENDACITY	REMONSTRANCE	PEDANTIC	BILIOUS	PLINTH
SOMNAMBULIST	PRODIGAL	CONDESCENSION	MISCELLANEOUS	GUMPTION

Pygmalion Vocabulary

PEREMPTORILY	MISCELLANEOUS	AMIABLE	BILIOUS	BROUGHAM
PEDANTIC	SOMNAMBULIST	REPUDIATES	DOGMATICALLY	MAGNANIMOUS
TOGS	DEMEAN	FREE SPACE	FROWZY	MENDACITY
PRODIGAL	PLINTH	DEPRECIATING	IMPETUOUS	PURGATORY
ASUNDER	ZEPHYR	INCORRIGIBLE	REMONSTRANCE	CONDESCENSION

Pygmalion Vocabulary

CONDESCENSION	REMONSTRANCE	INCORRIGIBLE	ZEPHYR	ASUNDER
PURGATORY	IMPETUOUS	DEPRECIATING	PLINTH	PRODIGAL
MENDACITY	FROWZY	FREE SPACE	DEMEAN	TOGS
MAGNANIMOUS	DOGMATICALLY	REPUDIATES	SOMNAMBULIST	PEDANTIC
BROUGHAM	BILIOUS	AMIABLE	MISCELLANEOUS	PEREMPTORILY

Pygmalion Vocabulary

SOMNAMBULIST	AMIABLE	INCORRIGIBLE	MISCELLANEOUS	REPUDIATES
CONDESCENSION	PURGATORY	PRODIGAL	MAGNANIMOUS	BILIOUS
PEREMPTORILY	DEPRECIATING	FREE SPACE	PEDANTIC	ZEPHYR
MENDACITY	DEMEAN	ASUNDER	PLINTH	IMPETUOUS
BROUGHAM	GUMPTION	DOGMATICALLY	TOGS	FROWZY

Pygmalion Vocabulary

FROWZY	TOGS	DOGMATICALLY	GUMPTION	BROUGHAM
IMPETUOUS	PLINTH	ASUNDER	DEMEAN	MENDACITY
ZEPHYR	PEDANTIC	FREE SPACE	DEPRECIATING	PEREMPTORILY
BILIOUS	MAGNANIMOUS	PRODIGAL	PURGATORY	CONDESCENSION
REPUDIATES	MISCELLANEOUS	INCORRIGIBLE	AMIABLE	SOMNAMBULIST

Pygmalion Vocabulary

FROWZY	IMPETUOUS	DEPRECIATING	GUMPTION	REPUDIATES
DEMEAN	PLINTH	TOGS	AMIABLE	SOMNAMBULIST
MISCELLANEOUS	MAGNANIMOUS	FREE SPACE	DOGMATICALLY	INCORRIGIBLE
PEREMPTORILY	MENDACITY	ZEPHYR	BROUGHAM	ASUNDER
PURGATORY	PRODIGAL	PEDANTIC	CONDESCENSION	BILIOUS

Pygmalion Vocabulary

BILIOUS	CONDESCENSION	PEDANTIC	PRODIGAL	PURGATORY
ASUNDER	BROUGHAM	ZEPHYR	MENDACITY	PEREMPTORILY
INCORRIGIBLE	DOGMATICALLY	FREE SPACE	MAGNANIMOUS	MISCELLANEOUS
SOMNAMBULIST	AMIABLE	TOGS	PLINTH	DEMEAN
REPUDIATES	GUMPTION	DEPRECIATING	IMPETUOUS	FROWZY

Pygmalion Vocabulary

DOGMATICALLY	REPUDIATES	DEPRECIATING	PEREMPTORILY	IMPETUOUS
FROWZY	GUMPTION	PRODIGAL	PEDANTIC	MAGNANIMOUS
MENDACITY	AMIABLE	FREE SPACE	BROUGHAM	DEMEAN
SOMNAMBULIST	INCORRIGIBLE	TOGS	BILIOUS	CONDESCENSION
PLINTH	REMONSTRANCE	MISCELLANEOUS	ZEPHYR	ASUNDER

Pygmalion Vocabulary

ASUNDER	ZEPHYR	MISCELLANEOUS	REMONSTRANCE	PLINTH
CONDESCENSION	BILIOUS	TOGS	INCORRIGIBLE	SOMNAMBULIST
DEMEAN	BROUGHAM	FREE SPACE	AMIABLE	MENDACITY
MAGNANIMOUS	PEDANTIC	PRODIGAL	GUMPTION	FROWZY
IMPETUOUS	PEREMPTORILY	DEPRECIATING	REPUDIATES	DOGMATICALLY

Pygmalion Vocabulary

DEPRECIATING	PURGATORY	MENDACITY	REMONSTRANCE	ASUNDER
INCORRIGIBLE	MISCELLANEOUS	TOGS	MAGNANIMOUS	GUMPTION
PRODIGAL	AMIABLE	FREE SPACE	PLINTH	ZEPHYR
DEMEAN	IMPETUOUS	PEREMPTORILY	DOGMATICALLY	BROUGHAM
FROWZY	PEDANTIC	BILIOUS	CONDESCENSION	SOMNAMBULIST

Pygmalion Vocabulary

SOMNAMBULIST	CONDESCENSION	BILIOUS	PEDANTIC	FROWZY
BROUGHAM	DOGMATICALLY	PEREMPTORILY	IMPETUOUS	DEMEAN
ZEPHYR	PLINTH	FREE SPACE	AMIABLE	PRODIGAL
GUMPTION	MAGNANIMOUS	TOGS	MISCELLANEOUS	INCORRIGIBLE
ASUNDER	REMONSTRANCE	MENDACITY	PURGATORY	DEPRECIATING

Pygmalion Vocabulary

PEDANTIC	PLINTH	AMIABLE	MAGNANIMOUS	DEPRECIATING
REMONSTRANCE	PEREMPTORILY	DEMEAN	BILIOUS	TOGS
INCORRIGIBLE	MISCELLANEOUS	FREE SPACE	FROWZY	PURGATORY
PRODIGAL	BROUGHAM	MENDACITY	REPUDIATES	ZEPHYR
DOGMATICALLY	CONDESCENSION	IMPETUOUS	SOMNAMBULIST	GUMPTION

Pygmalion Vocabulary

GUMPTION	SOMNAMBULIST	IMPETUOUS	CONDESCENSION	DOGMATICALLY
ZEPHYR	REPUDIATES	MENDACITY	BROUGHAM	PRODIGAL
PURGATORY	FROWZY	FREE SPACE	MISCELLANEOUS	INCORRIGIBLE
TOGS	BILIOUS	DEMEAN	PEREMPTORILY	REMONSTRANCE
DEPRECIATING	MAGNANIMOUS	AMIABLE	PLINTH	PEDANTIC

Pygmalion Vocabulary

CONDESCENSION	GUMPTION	DEPRECIATING	PRODIGAL	PEDANTIC
PEREMPTORILY	TOGS	REMONSTRANCE	PLINTH	BILIOUS
SOMNAMBULIST	MENDACITY	FREE SPACE	REPUDIATES	PURGATORY
FROWZY	MAGNANIMOUS	DEMEAN	IMPETUOUS	ASUNDER
ZEPHYR	INCORRIGIBLE	DOGMATICALLY	AMIABLE	BROUGHAM

Pygmalion Vocabulary

BROUGHAM	AMIABLE	DOGMATICALLY	INCORRIGIBLE	ZEPHYR
ASUNDER	IMPETUOUS	DEMEAN	MAGNANIMOUS	FROWZY
PURGATORY	REPUDIATES	FREE SPACE	MENDACITY	SOMNAMBULIST
BILIOUS	PLINTH	REMONSTRANCE	TOGS	PEREMPTORILY
PEDANTIC	PRODIGAL	DEPRECIATING	GUMPTION	CONDESCENSION